THE TWILIGHT OF THE
SUPREME COURT

THE TWILIGHT OF THE SUPREME COURT

A HISTORY OF OUR CONSTITUTIONAL THEORY

BY

EDWARD S. CORWIN, 1878-1963

ARCHON BOOKS
1970

SBN: 208 00839 X
Library of Congress Catalog Card Number: 73-103995
Printed in the United States of America

TO

THE MEMORY OF MY DEAR FRIEND

FRANCIS X. CARMODY

WITH WHOM I DISCUSSED

MANY OF THE QUESTIONS

HEREIN DEALT WITH

I INSCRIBE THIS VOLUME

CONTENTS

ACKNOWLEDGMENTS

In the following pages I have drawn as I found desirable upon certain previous studies of mine, for consenting to which procedure I wish to thank the editors and publishers of the *American Historical Review*, the *Cornell Law Quarterly*, the *Harvard Law Review*, the *Michigan Law Review*, and the *University of Pennsylvania Law Review*. My indebtednesses in this respect are indicated more specifically in footnotes at the appropriate points. I wish also to express my appreciation to my friends and colleagues, Professor Alpheus T. Mason and Dr. Paul T. Stafford, for reading this volume in proof; to the officers and staff of the Yale University Press, not only for the excellent way in which they have done their part, but for their unfailing patience with the author; and finally, and especially, to Dean Clark for his interest, counsel, and encouragement at all stages.

EDWARD S. CORWIN

Princeton University,
October 23, 1934.

FOREWORD

IT was indeed fortunate that the Yale School of Law was able just at this time to present upon its Storrs Lectureship Foundation the informing analyses given permanent form in this book. During its nearly fifty years of existence that lectureship has brought forth many distinguished contributions to constitutional theory and jurisprudence from both scholars and jurists. But rarely, if ever, has there occurred the remarkable union found in this book of these two fields, to the same vast illumination of the American theory of government, as well as of the "nature of the judicial process"—to borrow Justice Cardozo's famous phrase from another Storrs lecture. These lectures become available to the general reader at a time when public interest is perhaps more thoroughly aroused than ever before to the nature of our national government and its powers and duties with respect to the control and support of its citizens. Thousands of people are interested, if not concerned, as to the underlying validity of the extraordinary measures taken by the President and the Congress to meet the present crisis. The history of constitutional theory, so acutely presented here, suggests the answer. Despite the timeliness, however, of the publication, it will be apparent at once that these essays are not at all fashioned to make a momentary popular appeal, but are the matured conclusions of wise and sound scholarship on the history and present status of the most important as well as the most recurrent problems of our government.

This is not a new field for the distinguished author, but is, in fact, the one of which he long ago made himself master. His writings on American constitutional history and political theory are recognized as the authoritative expositions of the subject. After undergraduate and graduate study at the Universities of Michigan and Pennsylvania, respectively, he came to Princeton in 1905 as one of the original group of preceptors called there by President Wilson, and has remained there ever since—as Professor of Politics in 1911, and since 1918 as McCormick Professor of Jurisprudence. His essays dealing with constitutional theory include: *National Supremacy —Treaty Power vs. State Power* (1913), *The Doctrine of Judicial Review* (1914), *The President's Control of Foreign Relations* (1917), *John Marshall and the Constitution* (1919), *The Constitution and What It Means Today* (1920, 4th ed. 1930), and *The President's Removal Power* (1927). In addition to these books he has written many scholarly essays in legal, historical, and political science reviews—all of which have yielded their fruits to make possible the brief but masterly synthesis of the whole subject developed here.

It would be idle for me to attempt to summarize these lectures, but I should like to point out why I regard them as a new and important contribution to a field often traversed previously, not only by Professor Corwin but by hosts of other scholars. These lectures are unusual in that they weave together the various strands of American constitutional doctrines to form one central pattern, in which they all find their place. Taking as his central problem that of establishing a national power commensurate with the national scope of our economy, the author considers each of our important constitutional theories in its bearing upon this problem and in the light of the various shifts in approach to it made by our jurists at different times of our history. First we find the initial contrast between Hamilton's view of a strong national power and Madison's view of a compact of states—so aptly termed "dual federalism" by the author—with Hamilton's theory triumphing and being given abiding form by Marshall. Athwart this doctrinal development come, however, the different trends resulting from the expansion of the country after the Civil War and the growing feeling, finding reflection in the Court, that national well-being depended upon individual initiative and economic *laissez faire* in developing the country's resources. Hence the property-right concept, for which the Court had been seeking protection under the doctrine of vested rights or the idea of natural law, found a more or less permanent safeguard in the due process clause at the same time that the Court gave longing glances at the dual federalism of Madison and did, in fact, definitely assert it in the famous Child Labor Case (*Hammer* v. *Dagenhart*), subjected in the following pages to a devastating critique. But the economic fact was that business was national, that the states were powerless to check or control it, and that unless constitutional theory followed economic fact there would exist a no man's land between state and federal power not subject to any control. And so we have dual federalism and *laissez faire* both in full retreat before the Court's growing recognition that our present economic and social life cannot be compressed into separate state units. This is the subject matter of the first two lectures.

With the third lecture we meet the problem of the binding force of law and to whose hands should be given the function of changing it. Here it is made to appear how in the constitutional field in particular the functions of the Court have come to be more those of making law than of merely declaring it. This trend becomes more pronounced and more inevitable because of the increasing duplicity of our constitutional precedents touching the gravest questions of social purposes and ideals only slightly disguised as problems of constitutionality, with the result that decision becomes for the Court a matter of the freest choice. Along with this sharing by the Court of the work of the legislative department, accompanied by some jealousy of prerogative, has come an unusual expansion of the third great department of government, that of the Executive, with the approval, if not the actual coöperation, of the Court. All of this demonstrates that the doctrine of judicial review, or control of legislative action by our highest tribunal, has had unexpected results in hindering the development of national legislative action and in aiding the aggrandizement of the Presidency.

With the last lecture, however, comes the dénouement, which, as Dr. Corwin so strikingly points out, gives a sense of unreality, if not of futility, to the entire institution of judicial review as well as its product, constitutional law. It is the breakdown of all constitutional limitations found in the exercise of the spending power. Even from the beginning the spending power of the national government, though at times questioned in theory, has been steadily exercised throughout the country for all sorts of objects, until now this government may make itself "the universal and exclusive creditor of private business," or may even go into any business whatever, and the Supreme Court has held that there is no one to object. Neither taxpayer nor individual state has sufficient interest to be heard. If the national power may do all these things without let or hindrance, is it not unreal to have the regulation of private business "constantly frustrated by the courts in the name of 'due process,' the 'federal equilibrium,' or what not"?

Professor Corwin's final penetrating suggestion is

that, if the Court intended thus inconsiderately to refuse to relieve us of the responsibilities of popular
government as regards public expenditures, we might
have been better prepared to face these responsibilities, with more wisdom from experience, had it permitted us to face from the beginning the logical consequences of political democracy in the other field of
regulation of industry.

So far as the present recovery legislation and no-
tably the National Industrial Recovery Act are concerned, Professor Corwin indicates his general sympathy with the objectives of this legislation and from
time to time points out how they are in line with the
present trends of constitutional theory. In the main,
however, he allows history "to teach by example" (to
quote another famous Storrs lecturer, Professor Carl
Becker, in *The Heavenly City of the Eighteenth-
Century Philosophers*) and he does not attempt the
rôle of prophet. The lesson, however, is not less clear
and pointed for its urbane restraint. Judicial review,
so far as it has been an attempt on the part of the
Court to declare policies as to social developments,
has been hampering in those fields of governmental
regulation of industry where it has been tried. It has
kept national power lagging behind the actual fact
of economic organization. Meanwhile, however, in the
even more important field of governmental expenditure for all sorts of schemes and plans, it has been
powerless and futile. And the more this is apparent,

not only to students of constitutional history but to lawyers and to the Court itself, the less will be the willingness to risk the prestige of that most venerated body in further attempts at control and direction of social institutions. After all, is it a sound and practical theory, as well as a robust and vigorous doctrine, suited to an independent people, to hold that control and direction of its future should be committed to an aloof judicial tribunal, however esteemed? The teaching from experience, as developed in this wise little book, furnishes, it seems to me, the clear answer.

CHARLES E. CLARK

New Haven, Connecticut,
  October 8, 1934.

INTRODUCTION

THE New Deal has raised questions of constitutional power of a scope unapproached since the era of the Civil War and Reconstruction. Naturally, various attitudes have disclosed themselves, depending on the education, interests, what-not, of the persons concerned, but referable often, more or less, to different conceptions of the Constitution.

First of all there is the conception of the "man in the street." It consists, briefly, of a vague mental picture of a document which he has most probably never read through, but which he has been taught to believe contains clear-cut answers to all possible questions respecting governmental power in the United States. President Roosevelt is evidently of opinion that this conception may be profitably appealed to and hence is worth cultivating and improving. In his radio speech of June 28 he asked everybody to

answer this question out of the facts of your own life: Have you lost any of your rights of liberty or constitutional freedom of action and choice? Turn to the Bill of Rights of the Constitution, which I have solemnly sworn to maintain and under which your freedom rests secure. Read each provision of that Bill of Rights and ask yourself whether you personally have suffered the impairment of a single jot of these great assurances. I have no doubt as to what your answer will be.

In other words, it is the President's belief that if

everybody will but read the Constitution everybody will say at once that the New Deal is constitutional. Therein, I am persuaded, he is considerably in error. Almost anybody who knows no more
about the Constitution than the average American
voter does will in all likelihood conclude a reading
of that document with exactly the same views regarding the constitutionality of the New Deal as
he held when he began his novel intellectual exercise. Or, if this be something of an exaggeration,
at least it can be said that anyone who was convinced to begin with that he had lost his "rights of
liberty" in consequence of the New Deal would not
relinquish his grievance after reading the Bill of
Rights. For does it not say there in so many words
that "no person shall be deprived of liberty"? To
be sure, the prohibition is qualified by something
about "due process of law"; but can anything be
considered to be "due process of law" which de-
prives one of liberty? And in arguing thus, Mr.
Man-in-the-Street would have—quite unwittingly,
of course—summarized the practical significance
of one of the most important chapters in the history of constitutional interpretation in this country (see Chapter II, *infra*).[1]

Then there is also the view of the so-called "constitutional lawyer," that is to say, of almost any
member of the American Bar who still has hopes of
some day getting a case before the Supreme Court
of the United States. Many other countries, too—
most of them, in fact—have written constitutions,
but "the constitutional lawyer" is a unique prod-

uct of our system, whence no doubt the school-
boy's perspicacious description of it as "a government of lawyers and not of men."

The most interesting thing about the constitutional lawyer's conception of the Constitution is
that, except on certain state occasions like Constitution Day, it has very little to do with the constitutional document, which indeed becomes reduced
to little more than a taking-off place. To the professional mind "the Constitution" that is worth
talking about comprises judicial decisions purporting to interpret the constitutional document,
but more especially *those decisions in which some
national or state law has been declared "unconstitutional."* Nor is this strange, for usually the best
fees are to be had from those who have an interest
in resisting the extension of governmental authority; nor do the decisions in which challenged
legislation was sustained offer by any means the
same degree of promise of future litigation—and
hence of fees—that the other sort do.[2]

But while this attitude is explicable, it is not
necessarily commendable from a public point of
view, and even so conservative a jurist as Chief
Justice White took the opportunity to register his
disapproval of it. Said he:

There is great danger, it seems to me, to arise from the
constant habit which prevails where anything is opposed
or objected to, of resorting without rhyme or reason to
the Constitution as a means of preventing its accomplishment, thus creating the general impression that the Constitution is but a barrier to progress instead of being the

broad highway through which alone true progress may be enjoyed. Upon whom does the duty more clearly rest to modify and correct this evil than upon the members of our profession?[3]

And Justice McKenna, on one occasion, delivered himself of a similar homily in an opinion for the Court:

Against that conservatism of mind which puts to question every new act of regulating legislation and regards the legislation invalid or dangerous until it has become familiar, government—state and national—has pressed on in the general welfare; and our reports are full of cases where in instance after instance the exercise of regulation was resisted and yet sustained against attacks asserted to be justified by the Constitution of the United States. The dread of the moment having passed, no one is now heard to say that rights were restrained or their constitutional guaranties impaired.[4]

One recalls—perhaps Justice McKenna had in mind—Douglas Jerrold's description of a "conservative" as "a man who will not look at the new moon out of respect for that ancient institution the old one."

From the Bar we turn to the Bench, or more specifically to the Supreme Court, since its say regarding the metes and bounds of governmental power is apt to be final. Classified for their conceptions of the Constitution, Justices of the Supreme Court fall into two schools, the *old* and the *new*. The "old school" Justice took—and takes—his view of the Constitution, *up to a certain point*, from the common law, which he regards as a mysterious something whereof he, the judge, is the inspired mouthpiece. Confined to the common law, the view is a workable one, inasmuch as that law is acknowledged to have, in addition to its power to suffuse the minds of judges, also a power of growth and of adaptation to present needs. However, the very same judge who will one day be found lauding this flexibility of the common law, will be found the next day repudiating any such quality for the Constitution! Indeed, he will urge that, to claim such a quality for the Constitution would be to destroy the judicial quality of the judge. So long as he sticks to the common law, a judge can still be the mere mouthpiece of a law which grows and develops of itself, but in the field of the law of the Constitution, the case is entirely different.[5]

The theory of the automatism of the Court's rôle in relation to the Constitution has never been better expressed than in the following words of Justice Brewer, who was a member of the Court from 1889 to 1910. He assures us:

There is nothing in this power of the judiciary detracting in the least from the idea of a government of and by the people. . . . The courts hold neither purse nor sword; they cannot corrupt nor arbitrarily control. They make no laws, they establish no policy, they never enter into the domain of public action. They do not govern. Their functions in relation to the state are limited to seeing that popular action does not trespass upon right and justice as it exists in written constitutions and natural law. So it is that the utmost power of the courts and judges works no interference with true liberty, no trespass on the fullest and highest development of government of and by the people; it only means security to personal rights—the inalienable rights, life, liberty, and pursuit of happiness.[6]

Justice Brewer here assumes that the "liberty" protected by the Constitution is something definite, fixed, and clear, and that the judges know just what it is and will always act according to their knowledge. On the other hand, it can easily be shown that no Justice ever sat on the Supreme Bench who was more resolute than he to read his own social and economic theories into the Constitution and especially into the word "liberty" there. Nor is there any contradiction here between assumption and fact. Naturally, a conscientious judge who believes that his favorite dogmas are already in the Constitution will be most resolute in enforcing those dogmas as law of the land.

"Judges," remarked Justice Holmes, who had certainly known a number of them, "are apt to be naif, simple-minded men, and they need something of Mephistopheles. We too need education in the obvious—to learn to transcend our convictions and to leave room for much that we hold dear to be done away with short of revolution by the orderly change of law."[7] These words state the outlook of the "new school" Justice very adequately. Such a Justice is willing to believe that the bosom of the judge is not a vacuum from which everything except the law he is about to speak has been pumped; and furthermore, that in the present state of con-

stitutional law and theory, the compulsion which
rests upon him from the constitutional document
and from the Court's past decisions in interpretation thereof is very far indeed from being absolute.[8] And he is quite right, certainly in the latter
belief. *Its own freedom of decision is the outstanding product of the Court's exercise of the power of
judicial review,* as the following pages will demonstrate. It is, in fact, their principal message.

While the ensuing work purports to be chiefly
historical, I have no hesitation in avowing a sym-
pathetic interest in the larger features of the New
Deal, and especially in its wider-reaching implications, which I take to be as follows: first, that Business, being capable of affecting the lot in life of
most of us fully as much as Government itself, is
no longer to be considered a purely private enterprise; secondly, that "apart from some further di-
rective agency, mere individualistic competition, of
itself and by its own self-righting character," is
incapable of producing a satisfactory society;[9]
and finally that technological advances make it
more evident every day that the future relationship of the political to the economic forces of society is not to be determined solely on the basis of
inherited ideas. At the same time, I have not aimed
generally to extend my advocacy beyond an effort
to link up the constitutional principles upon which
the New Deal's validity would seem to depend, and
of which it may be therefore deemed declaratory,
to the more congenial trends of our constitutional
law and theory in the past.

"We are under a Constitution, but the Constitution is what the judges say it is."

GOVERNOR (now CHIEF JUSTICE) HUGHES.

CHAPTER I

DUAL FEDERALISM VERSUS NATIONALISM, AND THE INDUSTRIAL PROCESS

I.

DOES *the existence of the states furnish an independent determinant of, or limitation upon, national power?* Of the various questions with which constitutional law and theory have to deal touching the relations of the states and the national government this is the one of greatest practical consequence, as it is also one of the first to have been raised. It had emerged indeed, in implication at least, even before the adoption of the Constitution, in the pages of the *Federalist*.[1]

"The fabric of American empire," wrote Hamilton in *Federalist No. 22*, "ought to rest on the solid basis of the *Consent of the People*. The streams of national power ought to flow immediately from that pure, original fountain of all legitimate authority."[2] And from this premise ensued certain principles of interpretation of the powers of the proposed government. Because it was "impossible to foresee or define the extent and variety of national exigencies" as regards the national defense, "no constitutional shackles," says he, "can wisely be imposed on the power to which the care of it is committed." On this subject, therefore, "the government of the Union must be impowered to pass all laws"; and "the same must be the case in respect to commerce and to every other matter to which its jurisdiction is permitted to extend." "A government the constitution of which renders it unfit to be trusted with all the powers which a free people *ought to delegate to any government*, would be an unsafe and improper depositary of the NATIONAL INTERESTS." Turning then to the "necessary and proper" clause Hamilton answered the question, "Who is to judge the *necessity* and *propriety*" of acts of Congress, in these words: "The national government, like every other, must judge in the first instance of the proper exercise of its powers, and its constituents in the last." Later on, to be sure, in *Federalist No. 78*, Hamilton came to espouse the doctrine of judicial review, but only for the protection it promised to individual rights. That this device would be available also to safeguard the residual powers of the states he seems never to have recognized.

Regarding all these topics Madison's attitude is easily and significantly distinguishable. "The Constitution is to be founded," he wrote in *Federalist No. 39*, "on the assent and ratification of the people of America" given, however, "not as individuals composing one entire nation, but as composing the distinct and independent states to which they respectively belong. It is to be the assent and ratification of the several states, derived from the supreme authority in each state," and so would be a *federal* not a *national* act. It would, in other words, proceed from *already established po-*

litical entities, the states, not from the primitive
right of men to whose exercise these entities were
in turn ascribed in 1787.

Likewise, when Madison in this same number
comes to discuss the *extent* of the powers of the
proposed government, it is from the side of the
limitation which, he considers, will result from
the "residuary and inviolable sovereignty" of the
states; and his sole reference to judicial review is
to it as an agency for protecting this same inviolable sovereignty. The boundary between the two
jurisdictions will be "ultimately" decided, he asserts, by the Supreme Court; but in fact he later
suggests a still more "ultimate" recourse, and one
of a very different nature. "Should," he writes in
Federalist, No. 46, "an unwarrantable measure of
the federal government be unpopular in particular
states . . . the means of opposition to it are
powerful and at hand. The disquietude of the
people, the frowns of the executive magistracy of
the state, the embarrassments created by legislative devices . . . would oppose difficulties . . .
not to be despised." Nor would the opposition be
confined to single states. "Every government
would espouse the common cause. A correspond-
ence would be opened. Plans of resistance would be
concerted. . . ." The Madison of 1788 is already
within hailing distance of the Madison of 1798.[3]

From the point of view of our present interest
the period of Federalist domination, from 1789 to
1801, ought rather be termed the period of *nationalist* domination. The central core of Federalist

constitutional theory was the idea that the primary purpose of the Constitution was the establishment of an energetic and powerful national
government, any previous powers and preroga-
tives of the states to the contrary notwithstanding.
That Hamilton's legislative program should have
been elaborated in conformity with this idea is, of
course, not surprising; but even Madison conceded
at first the vital proposition that the question of
the scope of national power was one which should
be resolved independently of the consideration
that the states are recognized by the Constitution
as retaining certain powers. Thus, in the midst of
opposing Hamilton's Bank proposal as resting on
a strained construction of the enumerated powers
of Congress, he nevertheless remarked: "Interference with the powers of the states was no constitutional criterion of the power of Congress. If the
power was not given, Congress could not exercise
it; if given, they might exercise it, although it
should interfere with the laws or even the constitution of the States."[4] The "supremacy" clause was
still regarded as meaning what it says.

Such also was the outlook of the Supreme Court
of the period. In *Chisholm* v. *Georgia*[5] the Court
held, in the face of a positive assurance to the contrary by Hamilton in the *Federalist*, that its jurisdiction extended to a suit against a state by the
citizen of another state. Said Justice Wilson, "As
to the purposes of the Union Georgia is not a sovereign state";[6] while Jay advanced the contention,
to be later revived by Lincoln on the eve of the

Civil War, that the Union was older than the Constitution, older even than the states.[7] So far, indeed, was the Court of this period from considering the coexistence of the states as having any
bearing upon the problem of defining the powers
of the new government that it consistently rejected
every argument which might make difficult the employment of these powers for the benefit of the
country at large. The argument urged against the
Carriage Tax of 1795, that it was a "direct" tax
and hence should have been apportioned, the
Court answered by pointing out that a tax of that
nature could not be apportioned without producing absurd and unjust results. The purpose of the
"direct" tax clauses, the Court held, was a relatively limited one, and they should not, therefore,
be given an interpretation which would substantially attenuate the national taxing power.[8] And
the same point of view dictated the contemporary
decision in *Ware* v. *Hylton*,[9] upholding in sweeping terms the supremacy of national treaties over
both states' rights and vested rights.

Federalistic nationalism reached its climax in
the enactment of the Alien and Sedition Acts of
1798. The former was defended as springing from
the inherent right of the national community to
protect itself against undesired members, of which
right Congress, as the national legislature, was the
constitutionally authorized organ—an argument
which was ratified in detail by the Supreme Court
a century later in the Chinese Exclusion Cases.[10]
The Sedition Act carried the self-protective prin-

ciple still farther, finding it inherent in the organization of the *government* itself when considered in the light of principles of the common law.

This time, however, the partisans of nationalism overreached themselves, and in the Virginia and Kentucky Resolutions of 1798 and 1799 a radically different conception of the Constitution found utterance. The Constitution was asserted to rest primarily on a compact among the "sovereign" states, its obligatory force over which was, therefore, ultimately a moral rather than a legal one. The conversion of this *moral* obligation into a simple tie of *convenience* still awaited the dissolving dialectic of Calhoun.

Sustained in the first instance by the narrowly localistic outlook of the numerous small-farmer class and later on by the interests of slavery, the theory of the Constitution as a compact of the state sovereignties became finally a gloss upon the written instrument dominating its interpretation in every field.[11] So far, however, as the Supreme Court was concerned, this development was postponed many years by the fortuitous—or providential—circumstance of Marshall's Chief-Justiceship. It may justly be said that Marshall's greatest service consisted precisely in the uphill fight which he maintained for years against the trend of his times. An accomplished debater and clothed with the authority of the highest of judicial offices, he was able to invest the constitutional creed of his party with enduring form. For once at least we have occasion to rejoice at the supposed propensity of courts for outmoded ideas.

Marshall's principles of constitutional construction touching the relation of national power to the states sum up as follows: The Constitution was derived from the American population and hence should be interpreted from the point of view securing to them the full benefit of its provisions and of the governmental powers which it calls into existence—a thought implicit in the "necessary and proper" clause. For the same reason the coexistence of the states was not a factor of national power, a thought implicit in the "supremacy" clause. It was also an essential element of the supremacy of the national government within its assigned field that it should be entitled to delimit that field through one of its own organs, to wit, the Supreme Court. Lastly, the Constitution was intended to "endure for ages to come," and hence to "be adapted to the various crises of human affairs," and the ultimate agency to perform this task of adaptation was also the Court.[12]

The completest exposition by Marshall of his constitutional creed on the side of nationalism is his celebrated opinion in *McCulloch* v. *Maryland*.[13] That famous pronouncement evoked a storm of hostile criticism from the jealous exponents of states rights, one which did not wholly abate until his death. But of much greater significance for our purposes is the criticism which Madison, now in retirement, proceeded to level against Marshall's

approach to questions of national power. With
"the father of the Constitution," concern for
states rights came at last to be subordinated to,
and involved with, another idea, that in dual federalism America had rendered a contribution to
political science and to human happiness that was
altogether unique. The federal system, he declared at this period, had succeeded "beyond any
of the forms, ancient and modern" with which it
might be compared. Its beneficent operation entitled Americans to the glory "of having solved for
the destinies of man the problem of his capacity
for self-government." It was "the best guardian
. . . of the liberty, the safety, and the happiness
of man." It was the best, if not the only, assurance
of the survival of "a government based on free
principles."[14]

His successor to the Presidency was of like opinion: "So great an effort in favor of human happiness was never made before; but it became those
who made it."[15] Also this was the period when De
Tocqueville visited these shores. Wrote this sym-
pathetic and discerning critic:

If the temper and manners of the inhabitants [of the
United States] especially fitted them to promote the welfare of a great republic, the federal system smoothed the
obstacles which they might have encountered. . . .
Within the frontiers of the Union the profoundest peace
prevails, as within the heart of some great empire;
abroad, it ranks with the most powerful nations of the
earth. . . . The Union is as happy and as free as a small
people, and as glorious and strong as a great nation.[16]

American federalism combined, in short, the possibility of national grandeur with the maintenance of liberal institutions.

Nor can it be overlooked that this "discovery" of the federal system took place in an era when the rapid spread westward of the Union and the coming to political consciousness, under the Jacksonian leadership, of the Frontier, taken in conjunction, conveyed a warning not to be ignored, that if our predestined appropriation of the Continent was to be effected without the breakup of the Union, the fortunate outcome would be due in no small measure to the inherent flexibility of American federalism. Federalism was unquestionably, as De Tocqueville's great continuator was to point out two generations later, an indispensable means in the achievement of the physical basis of our national existence.[17] Nor can its importance in this respect be said to have come definitely to an end much prior to 1900. By that date, however, not merely had "the frontier" disappeared as a concept of the map makers; the imposition upon the nation at large of the two great party organizations, of a uniform system of public education, and of a nation-wide system of communications had rendered pervasive among the great mass of the American people a common outlook, which was supported in the main by common standards of livelihood.

Returning, however, to the year 1820, we may well lend some sympathy to Madison's concern for the maintenance of "the balance between the states and the national government," and even with his contention that Marshall's doctrines of constitutional law were calculated to upset this. Their central vice, he asserted with reason, was to treat the powers of the general government as "sovereign powers," the inevitable tendency of which must be "to convert a limited into an unlimited government." For, he continued "in the great system of political economy, having for its general object the national welfare, everything is related immediately or remotely to every other thing; and, consequently, a power over any one thing, if not limited by some obvious and precise affinity, may amount to a power over every other." "The very existence," he consequently urged, "of the local sovereignties" was "a control on the pleas for a constructive amplification of national power."[18] In brief, the existence of the states *was* a criterion of national power, not so much in the interest of the states themselves, but because it underlay the greatest of all political inventions, was indeed the *sine qua non* of its survival.

Marshall's death occurred July, 1835, and within less than two years the Court was substantially remade, receiving a new Chief Justice and five new Associate Justices. Writing at this period, Justice Henry Baldwin paid tribute to the honesty of Marshall's method of constitutional construction and its historical solidity. "He never brought into action the powers of his mighty mind to find some meaning in plain words above the comprehension of ordinary minds. He knew the framers of the Constitution who were his compatriots," and so "knew its objects, its intentions." For all that, said Baldwin, "the history and spirit of the times, past and present, admonish us that new versions of the Constitution will be promulgated to meet the ever varying course of political events and aspirations of power."[19]

Volume XI of Peters' *Reports* amply vindicates Baldwin's discernment. Here occur three cases which involved crucial questions of state power, each of which had been heard by Marshall, and in each of which, according to the trustworthy testimony of Story, the Chief Justice had adjudged the state enactment involved to be unconstitutional, although no decision had been handed down because the Court was not of full membership. In Peters' Volume XI, each of these enactments was sustained by the new Bench in the 1837 term.[20]

The central conception of the Court under Taney affecting constitutional interpretation was that of *the federal equilibrium;* in other words, the idea that the then existing distribution of powers between the states and the national government should be regarded as something essentially fixed and unchangeable; while defending this central conception was a series of corollary outposts: First, the Constitution was primarily a compact of the peoples of the states and only secondarily a part of the law of each state, albeit unchangeable thereby so long as the compact lasted. Secondly, power in the United States was divided between two authorities of *equal* dignity, the states and the national government, both of which operated over a common territory and a common citizenship for distinct purposes. Thirdly, the peculiar field of the national government was that of external relationship; the peculiar field of the states, that of internal government. Fourthly, the powers of the former ought not, therefore, generally be construed in such a way as to project them into the interior of the states. Indeed, fifthly, the Tenth Amendment—a provision never mentioned by Marshall in connection with questions of national power—reserved a field of power to the states within which the principle of national supremacy was not intended to operate. Sixthly, the Constitution was static, speaking always "not only in the same words, but with the same meaning and intent" as when it came from its framers. Finally, in relation to the Constitution, the Supreme Court was not the instrument of a supreme national power but an impartial umpire between two seats of *equal* power, the states and the national government; speaking precisely, the "supremacy" of the national *government* was that of the *Court*.[21]

The famous Dred Scott decision and that in *Kentucky* v. *Dennison*[22] equally illustrate the approach of the Court of this period to questions of national power especially in the legislative field. In the former several of the Justices denied categorically that Congress had any independent power in the territories at all—its powers were merely those of trustee and agent for the co-proprietor states. In the latter, decided on the eve of the Civil War,

we find a unanimous Court assenting to the proposition that the "Federal Government under the
Constitution has no power to impose on a state official as such any duty whatever and compel him to
perform it," a doctrine which directly contradicts
Marshall's assertion in *Cohens* v. *Virginia*,[23] that
in effecting its purposes the government of the
Union "may legitimately control all individuals or
governments within the American territory."

Off the Bench even extremer tendencies found
official expression. Thus, when in November, 1860,
President Buchanan put the question to Attorney-
General Black whether the general government
would be constitutionally warranted in attempting
to enforce its laws within the boundaries of states
claiming to have seceded from the Union, the answer returned was negative. The Attorney-General
asserted that the Constitution knew no such thing
as insurrection against the United States, and
hence made no provision for it, that the only insurrection with which the general government was em-
powered to deal was insurrection against individual states.[24] Buchanan's Message of December
3 did not go so far as this, but arrived at equally
paradoxical conclusions.[25] Seward's contemporary
comment was that the President had proved that
"no state had a right to secede—unless it wished
to" and that "the United States had the right to
enforce its laws—unless they were resisted."

The depleted condition to which the prevalent
theory of the Constitution had reduced national
power by 1861 could hardly have been more viv-

idly demonstrated than by Lincoln's course at the outset of the Civil War in falling back upon the then untested powers of the President as commander-in-chief rather than upon the powers of Congress. The War itself, to be sure, restored the conception of the national government as a territorial sovereignty, present in the states of its own right and capable of executing "on every foot of American soil the powers and functions that belong to it";[26] despite which the theory of dual federalism still remained for some years the most potential concept of the jurisprudence of the Court. Instructive in this connection is the case of *Collector* v. *Day*,[27] in which it was held that a national income tax, otherwise entirely constitutional, was not collectible on the official salary of a state judge. Invoking "the separate and independent condition of the states in our complex system," the Court remarked: "The supremacy of the general government, therefore, so much relied upon by counsel for the plaintiff in error, in respect to the question before us, cannot be maintained. The two governments are upon an equality. In respect to the reserved powers, the state is as sovereign and independent as the general government." In the contemporaneous Slaughter House[28] and Civil Rights cases[29] construction of the recently adopted Fourteenth Amendment was at first entirely swayed by the idea of preserving the federal equilibrium intact and unchanged from what the Court imagined it to have been always. In the latter cases the controlling opinion frankly subordinates the later amendment to the Tenth Amendment, and the total result of the two decisions was to postpone for some years the nationalization of private rights which the amendment was unquestionably intended by its authors to bring about.

So by the year 1885, or thereabouts, American constitutional law and theory had come to embrace two widely divergent although equally well matured traditions regarding national power. The one tradition insists on the adaptability of national power to "an undefined and expanding future" and leaves the maintenance of the federal system and of states rights largely contingent thereon; in the words of Justice Holmes, it recognizes that the Constitution has to "take some chances." The other tradition erects dual federalism into a supreme constitutional value, the preservation of which ought forever to control constitutional interpretation. And having these two traditions at hand, the Court became enabled in later decades, without too evident derogation from its judicial rôle, to frame responses from either when confronted with questions of national power. How, in fact, did it use its liberty? For many reasons the question is especially important in relation to Congress' power to regulate interstate commerce.

II.

THE first case to reach the Court under the "commerce" clause was *Gibbons* v. *Ogden*[30] in 1824. In deciding *Cohens* v. *Virginia* three years prior

Marshall had declared: "That the United States form for many and for important purposes a single nation, has not yet been denied. In war, we are one people. In making peace, we are one people. In all commercial regulations, we are one and the same people."[31] In *Gibbons* v. *Ogden* he yields the reluctant admission that the Constitution intends a distinction between "that commerce which concerns more states than one" and "the exclusively internal commerce of a state"; but he proceeds forthwith to pare away the force of this concession on all sides. "Commerce," he asserts, is not merely *"traffic,"* its primary significance; it is also "intercourse," and hence comprehends *navigation*, which is to say, transportation. "The power to regulate" is the power "to prescribe the rule by which commerce is to be governed," and

is vested in Congress as absolutely as it would be in a single government, having in its Constitution the same restrictions on the exercise of power as are found in the Constitution of the United States. The wisdom and the discretion of Congress, their identity with the people, and the influence which their constituents possess at elections are, in this, as in many other instances, as that, for example of declaring war, the sole restraints on which they have relied, to secure them from its abuse. They are the restraints on which the people must often rely solely, in all representative governments.[32]

In short, this power was in no wise affected by the coexistence of the states; was indeed the same as if there were no states. Nor was it confined by state lines, for it might be "exercised whenever the subject exists." Furthermore, it was a favorite canon of constitutional construction of Marshall's that "questions of power do not depend upon the degree to which it is exercised. If it exists at all, it may be exercised to the utmost extent"[33]—a maxim which necessarily infers that power may be exercised for whatever purposes those who wield it may choose to forward. As Webster expressed the idea in his argument for Gibbons, "there is no limit to . . . power to be derived from the *purpose* for which it is exercised. . . . No one can inquire into the *motives* which influence sovereign authority."[34] Indeed, it was only within recent years that the Court itself ever countenanced, and then perhaps but tentatively, a different theory in the field of national power.[35]

But once again we find Madison filing a demurrer to the Chief Justice's doctrines. Writing a friend in 1829, the former asserted that, although conferred in the same words as the power over foreign commerce, Congress' power over "commerce among the states" "was intended as a negative and preventive provision against injustice among the states themselves, rather than as a power to be used for the positive purposes of the general government, in which alone, however, the remedial power could be lodged."[36] The idea which Madison thus set going has had a varied history. Before the Civil War advocates of slavery welcomed the Madisonian dictum as protective of the interstate slave trade.[37] After the war, and during the period when the "commerce" clause was being erected into a broad-gauge restriction on state power, the Court repudiated the dictum.[38] But still later we find Justice White, latter-day hierophant of dual federalism, turning again to the dictum for its limiting effect on the national legislative power, and doing so apparently with the Court's entire approval,[39] albeit that body had meantime subscribed to the manifestly opposed doctrine that "the reasons which caused the framers of the Constitution to repose the power to regulate interstate commerce in Congress do not affect or limit the power itself."[40]

But whatever may be thought of the dictum as history, it turned out to be surprisingly good prophecy for many years. Following upon Marshall's death, the "commerce" clause, so far as it relates to interstate commerce, came to owe its importance in the cases for nearly two generations almost entirely to the doctrine, finally ratified by the Court in 1851, that Congress' power over commerce among the states is, as to matters of primary importance, an exclusive power,[41] and hence constitutes a restriction on state power even when Congress has not acted. The doctrine was first stated with substantial qualifications, but following the Court's indoctrination in the late eighties in the precepts of capitalistic *Laissez Faire*, these were largely cast aside, and the doctrine became, second only to the "due process" clause of the Fourteenth Amendment, the most important constitutional recourse of the new dispensation.

Responding to this fillip the Court's conception

of what is "commerce among the states" and as such entitled to judicial protection against state regulation, expanded markedly. Transportation within a state of goods destined to, or brought from, another state was held to be such commerce; also the sale by sample of goods to be brought from another state; also the sale of goods in a state for an assured market in another state.[42] These results were reached mainly in cases which involved state taxation measures. But in the Liquor, Cigarette, and Oleomargarine Cases, the Court laid down the further rule that a state could not forbid the entrance within its limits, at least without the consent of Congress, of "good articles of commerce" (that is to say, of articles found by itself to be "good"), nor their sale in the "original package."[43] Finally, by still another line of cases, no state may endeavor to promote its own internal prosperity by placing an embargo upon the flow of its products to other states,[44] the reason being that "in matters of foreign and interstate commerce, there are no state lines; in such commerce, instead of the states, a new power and a new welfare appear that transcend the power and welfare of any state."[45]

In brief, in the very act of safeguarding the development of interstate commerce from interruption by the states, the Court unavoidably built up an enlarged conception of the subject matter which the "commerce" clause in express words subjects to Congress' power to regulate. On the other hand, it built up at the same time a greatly mitigated conception of the word "regulate." It ceased to think of this power in the terms which Marshall had laid down, as the power to *govern*. Instead, it tended to view Congress' power under the "commerce" clause in the same light as it did its own, namely, as primarily a power to *foster, protect, and promote commerce.*[46] And so proceeding, the Court converted the clause into a broad highway for business to overspread the country without regard to state lines, and thus to effect an organization which has put itself beyond effective state control. Nevertheless, when Congress, discovering what was happening, endeavored belatedly to follow along this same highway it found itself confronted at every turn with the sign "no thoroughfare," erected ostensibly to safeguard state power and the principle of dual federalism.

The first distinct confrontation of the power to regulate commerce in the sense of governing it with *laissez faire* occurred in the Sugar Trust Case of 1895,[47] involving the Sherman Anti-Trust Act of 1890. By the transaction under adjudication, the Court admitted, the defendant company had acquired "nearly complete control of the manufacture of refined sugar in the United States." For all that, the Court ruled, the act could not constitutionally reach the case. Said Chief Justice Fuller, speaking for the Court:

It is vital that the independence of the commercial power and of the police power, and the delimitation between them, however sometimes perplexing, should always be recognized and observed, for while the one furnishes the strongest bond of union, the other is essential to the preservation of the autonomy of the states as required by our dual form of government; and acknowledged evils, however grave and urgent they may appear to be, had better be borne, than the risk be run, in the effort to suppress them, of more serious consequences by resort to expedients of even doubtful constitutionality.[48]

Following this exordium, the Court proceeded to hold that the object of the combination before it was "private gain in the manufacture of the commodity," and that manufacture was a purely local process. To be sure, it conceded, the product was sold and distributed among the states, "but this was no more than to say that trade and commerce served manufacture to fulfil its function"![49] Thus was commerce in its primary sense of *traffic*, of buying and selling, simply and with astonishing casualness, wiped out of the constitutional grant of power! What, then, was left for Congress to govern? Only "the final movement" of goods "from their state of origin to that of destination" —interstate *transportation*, in short. As we shall see in a moment, even this concession was presently seriously qualified.

Eight years after the Sugar Trust Case the famous Lottery Case (*Champion* v. *Ames*)[50] reached the Court, raising the question of the validity of the act of 1895 penalizing the carriage of lottery tickets from one state to another. The assailants of the act revived the contention that Congress' power over commerce was merely a power to foster and promote commerce; but they supplemented this argument, so far as interstate commerce was concerned, with the further contention that under the federal system the major objectives of government, the protection of the public health, safety, and morals, and the advancement of the general welfare—*other than commercial welfare*—fell exclusively to the police powers of the states. The act of 1895 was thus an invasion of a field of power which was unconditionally reserved to the states. By the same token, it menaced the federal principle.

That the Court found the case a difficult one is shown by the fact that it was thrice argued and that the decision finally sustaining the act was rendered by a vote of five Justices to four. Furthermore, later examination was to disclose that Justice Harlan's opinion for the majority was susceptible of a narrower as well as a broader explanation. Thus on the one hand the act of Congress is vindicated as being for the purpose of "guarding the people of the United States against 'the widespread pestilence of lotteries,' " language which infers that Congress may *prohibit* commerce when it believes that by doing so it can advance any of the usual purposes of good government. Yet on the other hand the measure is also justified as designed to *protect commerce* against "pollution" from lottery tickets—which reflects again the notion of the power to regulate commerce as simply the power to foster and promote it.[51]

Despite this ambiguity, Justice Harlan's opinion afforded at first much encouragement to those who, in increasing numbers, were planning on making of the "commerce" clause a fulcrum for social reforms of various kinds.[52] The earliest proposal for a federal anti-child labor act dates from this period; as does also the suggestion that Congress was entitled to require companies engaging in interstate commerce to take out a federal license or even a federal charter, proposals which were supported successively by President Roosevelt and President Taft. It was also doubtless owing to such encouragement that the Federal Employer's Liability Act as originally passed applied to all employees of interstate carriers, whether such employees were themselves engaged in interstate commerce or not. Dual federalism seemed about to pass into eclipse beneath the waxing orb of the commerce power. That it did not was due to no single cause more evidently than to the fervent championship of Justice White.

White's ascendancy with his colleagues is sufficiently attested by their unprecedented course at Fuller's death in petitioning President Taft to make White Chief Justice. Nor is the explanation far to seek. In its blended charm and force White's personality recalls the great Marshall himself. As a stylist he is, on the other hand, entirely unique. His lumbering sentences, clause piled on clause, phrase involuted within phrase, still manage to pulse with an insistent advocacy. Nor does he permit himself to be cramped by the nicer rules of controversy. He has no hesitancy about misstating an argument which he intends to reject; some of his own arguments are no better than a crude sort of punning; the ferocity with which he assails the straw men of his own creation can be comic.[53] His matter, too, is occasionally distinctive. A Catholic, educated in Jesuit schools, he not infrequently affords in his opinions striking confirmation to the traceable affiliations of American constitutional theory with the political thought of the Middle Ages, as in his famous "rule of reason" and in his repeated invocation of the notion of "inherent" powers and "inherent" limitations. Nor is it unlikely that his ardent espousal of the cause of dual federalism may also have owed something to acquaintance with its medieval counterpart, the dual jurisdiction over common territory of Church and Empire.

White's initial tilt on behalf of dual federalism (and incidentally of *laissez faire*) occurs in his dissenting opinion in the Northern Securities Case.[54] Here it was held that a company which through purchase of stock had acquired a dominating position in two competing railway systems, was a combination violative of the Sherman Act. This result, White asserted, tended to

extend the power of Congress to all subjects essentially local. . . . Under this doctrine the sum of property to be acquired by individuals or by corporations, the contracts which they may make, would be within the regulating power of Congress. If it were judged by Congress that the farmer in sowing his crops should be limited to a certain production because over-production would give

power to affect commerce, Congress could regulate that
subject.

The result of such a principle, he continued,

would be not only to destroy the state and federal governments, but by the implication of authority from which
the destruction would be brought about, there would be
erected upon the ruins of both a government endowed
with arbitrary power to disregard the great guaranty of
life, liberty and property and every other safeguard upon
which organized civil society depends.[55]

In its prevision of certain measures of the New
Deal and its reiteration of Madison's conception
of dual federalism as a necessary support of liberal government, this passage contrives to con-
front the future with the past in a rather surprising way.

In the first Employers' Liability Cases,[56] White
the dissentient became the spokesman of the Court.
The Government in defending the act of 1906 contended, in reliance on its recent victories in the
Lottery Case and the Northern Securities Case,
that "one who engages in interstate commerce
thereby submits all his business concerns to the
regulating power of Congress." Justice White re-
torted in characteristic phrase:

To state the proposition is to refute it. It assumes that
because one engages in interstate commerce, he thereby
endows Congress with power not delegated to it by the
Constitution; in other words, the right to legislate concerning matters of purely state concern. . . . It is apparent that if the contention were well founded it would

extend the power of Congress to every conceivable subject, however inherently local, would obliterate all the
limitations of power imposed by the Constitution, and
would destroy the authority of the states as to all conceivable matters which, from the beginning, have been,
and must continue to be, under their control so long as
the Constitution endures.[57]

A year later, nevertheless, the Court was once
more faced by the same issue, at least in its own
belief.[58] The legislation involved forbade a carrier
to haul in interstate commerce articles or commodities in which it had "any interest direct or
indirect."[59] The question raised, asserted Justice
White, once more the Court's mouthpiece, was
"whether the power of Congress to regulate commerce embraces the authority to control or prohibit the mining, manufacturing, production or
ownership of an article or commodity, not because
of some inherent quality of the commodity, but
simply because it may become the subject of interstate commerce?" Approaching the enactment
from this angle, the Court gave to judicial review
a new extension. The provision was in form sustained, but under a construction which made it inapplicable to products of companies in which the
carrier owned stock, thereby avoiding, White explained, a "grave and doubtful constitutional
question."[60]

III.

From the above two decisions to that in the first
Child Labor Case (*Hammer* v. *Dagenhart*),[61] al-

though in point of time ten years divide them, is a single logical step. Here the Court, by a bare majority—which included White—held void the act of 1916, forbidding the shipment in interstate commerce of child-labor products. The opinion of the Court by Justice Day is so notable as an attempt to apply the concept of dual federalism in the presence of certain constitutional precedents, as well as present-day economic fact, as to warrant a somewhat careful examination.

The opinion boils down to three propositions: (1) that the act was *not* a regulation of commerce among the states; (2) that it *was* an invasion of powers reserved to the states; (3) that it was, therefore, inimical to the federal system which it was the design of the Constitution to set up and maintain. One evident difficulty here is to determine whether the second proposition should be regarded as dependent on the first or as having independent force of its own sufficient to invalidate the act of Congress. Assuming the second possibility, Justice Holmes in his dissenting opinion asserted that a statute "within the power expressly given to Congress if considered only as to its immediate effects" was being held invalid for its collateral effects within the normal field of state power. "I should have thought," said he, "that the most conspicuous decisions of this Court had made it clear that the power to regulate commerce and other constitutional powers could not be cut down or qualified by the fact that it might interfere with the carrying out of the domestic policy of any state,"[62] a position which is clearly incontrovertible except on the assumption that Justice Day's third proposition states a transcendental value which rises above and nullifies the express phraseology of the Constitution itself where the two conflict.

Waiving this question for the moment, however, let us turn to Justice Day's first proposition. The ground thereof is soon found to be the idea that a prohibition of commerce is not normally a regulation of it, because destructive of it. To be sure, Justice Day admits, there have been cases in which regulation legitimately took the form of prohibition, but, he contends,

in each of these instances the use of interstate transportation was necessary to the accomplishment of harmful results. . . . This element is wanting in the present case. . . . The goods shipped are in themselves harmless . . . when offered for shipment, and before transportation begins, the labor of production is over, and the mere fact that they were intended for interstate transportation does not make their production subject to federal control under the commerce clause.

Two quite distinct, and indeed conflicting, ideas are here intermingled, or confused: first, the idea that Congress may exclude from interstate transportation only things that are harmful *in themselves;* secondly, the idea that it may exclude objects the *transportation* of which is *followed* by harmful results. And not only are these ideas in conflict with each other, neither is valid as it is here applied.

To say that Congress may exclude from interstate commerce only objects that are harmful in themselves is to invoke the idea that any regulation of commerce must always be justified by an intention on the part of Congress to *protect* commerce itself, an idea which, as we have seen already, encounters the gravest historical and logical objections. Nor is this all; for the idea that Congress may exercise an express power given without qualification only for a certain purpose or certain purposes to be finally determined by the Court, is to endow the Court with the power to invalidate acts of Congress because of Congress' supposed purpose in passing them, something which Justice Day himself says may not be done—even in the act of doing it!

Moreover, Justice Day also admits that interstate transportation may be forbidden if it is followed by "harmful results," which means results *judged by the Court* to be harmful—which again is a palpable invasion of the field of legislative discretion. And it is an act of interstate *transportation* that must be followed by such results. That is to say, "commerce" is conceived as primarily *transportation*, and Congress' power over it is envisaged as beginning only with an act of transportation from one state to another; and from this it follows that Congress must shut its eyes to all "harmful results" which precede such act of transportation.

The first comment invited is, that in checking state power with the "commerce" clause, the Court has repeatedly treated Congress' power as operative before any act of transportation has started.[63] But furthermore, granting this conception of commerce, still a "harmful result" that followed transportation from one state to another would be just as much within the jurisdiction of the latter state as a harmful result which preceded the same act of transportation would be within the jurisdiction of the former state. Justice Day's argument therefore logically concedes that the fact that it reaches a subject matter which is within the normal jurisdiction of a state does not, of itself, suffice to invalidate an act of Congress.[64]

Yet again, the argument is directed to only one aspect of the Child Labor Act, which was intended not merely to repress child labor in certain states, but to prevent its spread through the operation of competition to other states. Justice Day himself recognizes this inadequacy of his argument, and proceeds to supplement it with following contention:

The commerce clause was not intended to give Congress a general authority to equalize conditions. In some of the states laws have been passed fixing minimum wage laws for women, in others the local law regulates the hours of labor of women in various employments. This fact does not give Congress the power to deny transportation in interstate commerce to those who carry on business where the hours of labor and the rate of compensation for women have not been fixed by a standard in use in other states and approved by Congress.

Not "a *general* authority" perhaps, but why not such authority as an otherwise valid exercise of its power to regulate commerce confers upon it? Certainly no words in the Constitution impose any such restriction upon Congress' power over commerce. On the contrary, the "commerce" clause, altogether independently of Congressional legislation under it, has been held by the Court repeatedly to forbid state legislation designed to give the enacting state an advantage in competition with sister states.[65] Why then should not Congress exercise the power which, after all, the Constitution confers upon *it* and not upon the Court, with the same objective in mind, and thereby equalize, if it can, conditions of competition among the states according to *its* views of sound social policy? Justice Day's assertion in denial once again invokes the unallowable assumption that the Court may supervise the purposes of Congress. It is the *sic volo, sic jubeo* of final authority, no less —but also no more.

The whole opinion of Mr. Justice Day rests moreover on the unallowable assumption that "commerce" is primarily *transportation*. As the etymology of the word reveals, it means primarily buying and selling, *traffic*, in brief. Indeed, in *Gibbons* v. *Ogden*, as we saw above, the crucial question was whether the term comprehended trans-

portation at all. And indubitably the correct
theory of the Child Labor Act is that it was designed to discourage a widespread and pernicious
traffic which both supported, and was supported
by, child labor in certain states, and which furnished a constant inducement to the spread of such
labor to other states. For without the interstate
market for its products child labor could not long
survive on any considerable scale. The act promised to be effective, in other words, not as a penalty
in terrorem, but by *eliminating the substantial
cause of the evil it struck at*. The Court's objection, therefore, that specific acts of production
precede specific acts of transporting the product
becomes frivolous; both these acts are but part
and parcel of something much broader, and that
something is interstate *commerce* in the original
understanding of the term.

We are thus brought to Justice Day's exalta-
tion of the Madisonian concept of dual federalism
as a superconstitutional value to which even the
express language of the Constitution must yield.
He says:

In interpreting the Constitution it must never be forgotten that the Nation is made up of States to which are
entrusted the powers of local government. And to them
and to the people the powers not expressly [*sic*] delegated to the National Government are reserved. *Lane
County v. Oregon,* 7 Wall. 71, 76. The power of the
States to regulate their purely internal affairs by such
laws as seem wise to the local authority is inherent and
has never been surrendered to the general government.

New York v. Miln, 11 Pet. 102, 139;[66] *Slaughter House Cases,* 16 Wall. 36, 63; *Kidd v. Pearson, supra.* . . . The far-reaching result of upholding the act cannot be more plainly indicated than by pointing out that if Congress can thus regulate matters entrusted to local authority by prohibition of the movement of commodities in interstate commerce, all freedom of commerce will be at an end, and the power of the States over local matters may be eliminated, and thus our system of government be practically destroyed. . . .[67]

Thus Justice Day ventures to amend the Tenth Amendment by interpolating in it the word "expressly"! And since Congress admittedly is not vested *expressly* with the power to prohibit the transportation of the products of child labor from one state to another, its attempt to do so becomes an invasion of the reserved powers of the states over "their purely internal affairs." But though the premise were sound, the conclusion would not follow. As Justice Holmes points out in his dissenting opinion for himself and three brethren, admitting the right of the states to control their *purely internal affairs,*

when they seek to send their products across the state line they are no longer within their rights. If there were no Constitution and no Congress their power to cross the line would depend upon their neighbors. Under the Constitution such commerce belongs not to the States but to Congress to regulate. It may carry out its views of public policy whatever indirect effect they may have upon the activities of the States. Instead of being encountered by a prohibitive tariff at her boundaries the State encoun-

ters the public policy of the United States which it is for
Congress to express. The public policy of the United
States is shaped with a view to the benefit of the nation
as a whole. . . . The national welfare as understood by
Congress may require a different attitude within its
sphere from that of some self-seeking State. It seems to
be entirely constitutional for Congress to enforce its understanding by all the means at its command.[68]

In other words, *Hammer* v. *Dagenhart* denies to
Congress power over commerce which originally
belonged to the individual states of the Union! As
a matter of fact, when read along with certain decisions in which the "commerce" clause has been
applied as a restraint on state power, it is found to
do something even more remarkable. By the plain
logic of the cases today neither Congress nor the
states, nor both together, can stop interstate commerce in the products of child labor. Such products being "good articles of commerce," no state
can prohibit their entry from another state nor
their sale in the original package within its boundaries, since to do so would be to invade the field of
Congress' power to regulate interstate commerce.[69]
But Congress, nevertheless, we are now informed,
may not exercise the power so solicitously entrusted
to its exclusive control, since to do so would be
to invade the field of power reserved to the states.
So the states, which, without challenge, originally
possessed this power, have now lost it by virtue of
having delegated it to Congress, but Congress has
never received it! "Dual federalism" thus becomes
triple federalism—inserted between the realm of

the national government and that of the states is one of no-government—a governmental vacuum, a political "no-man's land"; and this is in face of the Court's own repeated assurance that "the Constitution, whilst distributing the preëxisting power, preserved it all"![70]

Three subsequent cases cast further light on the logical and practical difficulties of this decision. In *United States* v. *Hill*,[71] decided within a twelve-month, the Court, speaking by the same Justice, sustained the Reed Bone-Dry Amendment to the Post Office Act of May 3, 1917, which prohibited the interstate transportation of intoxicants into states forbidding the manufacture and sale of the same. To the objection that if the provision was applied to liquors intended for personal use merely and not for sale, it conflicted with the laws of certain states, the Court answered:

Congress may exercise this authority over interstate commerce in aid of the policy of the state if it sees fit. It is equally clear that the policy of Congress acting independently of the states may induce legislation without reference to the particular policy or law of any given state. . . . The control of Congress over interstate commerce is not to be limited by state laws.[72]

That is to say, it is no objection to an otherwise valid exercise by Congress of its power to prohibit commerce, that its purpose is to correct state policy rather than to support it.

Then in *Bailey* v. *Drexel Furniture Company*[73] the Court, in 1922, set aside a special tax by Congress upon the net profits of manufacturing concerns employing children under other than stated conditions. The opinion of Chief Justice Taft for the Court relies quite unequivocally on the canon of constitutional interpretation which is disavowed by Justice Day in *Hammer* v. *Dagenhart*, that a measure otherwise within the power of Congress may be invalidated in defense of the federal system because of the supposed purpose of Congress to govern a matter within the normal control of the states. Indeed, the Chief Justice's explanation of the decision in *Hammer* v. *Dagenhart* puts it also upon the same ground. He says:

When Congress threatened to stop interstate commerce in ordinary and necessary commodities, *unobjectionable as subjects of transportation,* and to deny the same to the people of a state in order to coerce them into compliance with Congress's regulation of state concerns, the Court said that this was not in fact regulation of interstate commerce, but rather that of state concerns and was invalid.[74]

In other words, the Court, finding itself confronted with a situation wherein it was unable longer to defend its conception of dual federalism except by giving judicial review an application which it had previously repudiated, was equal to the occasion.[75]

Finally, in 1925, in *Brooks* v. *United States,*[76] the Court upheld the Motor Vehicle Theft Act of 1919, which makes it a penal offense against the United States to transport in interstate commerce

a motor vehicle known to have been stolen, or to
"conceal, barter, sell, or dispose" of the same.
After what appears to be an entirely irrelevant review of previous cases, the Chief Justice notes "the
radical change in transportation" brought about
by the automobile, and the rise of "elaborately organized conspiracies for the theft of automobiles
. . . and their sale or other disposition" in another
police jurisdiction from the owner's. "This," the
opinion declares, "is a gross misuse of interstate
commerce. Congress may properly punish such interstate transportation by any one with knowledge
of the theft because of its harmful result and its
defeat of the property rights of those whose ma-
chines against their will are taken into another
jurisdiction."[77] In short, the act is sustained
chiefly as protective of owners of automobiles, that
is to say, of *interests in "the state of origin,"* and
this result is directly connected with the Court's
having taken notice of "elaborately organized conspiracies" for the theft and disposal of automobiles across state lines—that is, of a widespread
traffic in such property.

IV.

OBVIOUSLY, *Hammer* v. *Dagenhart* is today elbowed into rather narrow quarters. Moreover, it
may happen with a legal as with a military position which does not yield readily to assault, that it
may be turned. Let us, therefore, concede for the
sake of the argument that Congress may not use

any of its powers for the purpose of regulating child labor; that is to say, *from humanitarian and kindred motives*, that on that proposition dual federalism stands or falls! But let us suppose also that the Court could be convinced that in the long run child labor, and other industrial practices of which child labor may be taken to be typical, injured interstate commerce—what, in light of the cases, would be the result?

That the official defenders of the N.I.R.A. will have to answer this question, I entertain no doubt; and I suggest that they would do well to begin with such cases as *Southern Railway* v. *United States,* the Second Employer's Liability Cases, the Shreveport Case, *Wilson* v. *New, United States* v. *Ferger, C. B. & Q. Railway* v. *Wisconsin Commission,* and so on.[78] It is unnecessary here to review these holdings inasmuch as their general purport is sufficiently set forth by Chief Justice White in the Ferger Case. Here defendants in error, who had been indicted under a federal statute for issuing a false bill of lading on a fictitious shipment, set up the contention that Congress' power covered only genuine shipments in interstate commerce, with the result that defendants' fraud could be validly punished only under state law. Chief Justice White answered:

But this mistakenly assumes that the power of Congress is to be necessarily tested by the intrinsic existence of commerce in the particular subject dealt with instead of by the relation of that subject to commerce and its effect upon it. We say, mistakenly assumes, because we think it clear that if the proposition were sustained it would destroy the power of Congress to regulate, as obviously that power, if it is to exist, must include the authority to deal with obstructions to interstate commerce, and with a host of other acts which, because of their relation to and influence upon interstate commerce, come within the power of Congress to regulate, although they are not interstate commerce in and of themselves.[79]

Not only, therefore, has the Court, in enforcing Congress' power to *protect interstate commerce against obstruction*, defined commerce broadly— as we saw earlier; it has also accorded full operation to Marshall's conception of national supremacy, paying slight heed to those theories which in one way or another make state power a debilitating ingredient of national power. But let us next suppose that the "obstruction" to commerce arises from the acts of people who are engaged in it or are its beneficiaries, results indeed from the type of commerce which they think it most profitable to carry on; what then? The question brings us back once more to the Sherman Act, with respect to which *laissez faire* had from the outset found itself faced with a somewhat embarrassing dilemma.

In the Sugar Trust Case,[80] as we have seen, the provisions of the Sherman Act were practically confined to commerce in the sense of transportation, with the consequence that Congress' effort to protect commerce in the sense of traffic from monopolistic obstruction was frustrated for more than a decade. On the other hand, *laissez faire* itself professes abhorrence of monopoly; and this also was the attitude of the Court, being indeed grounded on the common law.[81] Still, the benefits of dual federalism were not lightly to be cast aside either. Indeed, what other concept of constitutional law and theory offered better promise of immunity from national control for a business set-up that could now, with little further aid from either the Constitution or the Court, thumb its nose at local legislative programs?

In *Swift and Company* v. *United States*,[82] decided in 1905, the Court, responding to the Roosevelt anti-trust crusade and to the views of new appointees, virtually overruled its decision and entirely discarded its reasoning in the Sugar Trust Case. The defendants, some thirty firms engaged in Chicago and other cities in the business of buying livestock in their stockyards, of converting it at their packing houses into fresh meat, and in the sale and shipment of such fresh meat to purchasers in other states, were charged under the Sherman Act with having entered into a combination to refrain from bidding against each other in the local markets, to fix prices at which they would sell there, to restrict shipments of meat, and to do other forbidden acts, and had been enjoined therefrom. Their appeal to the Supreme Court was based on the contention that the acts just recited were not acts of interstate commerce, and hence not within national jurisdiction. The Court, speaking by Justice Holmes, answered that, granting the acts were in themselves local, and hence subject to state regulation and taxation, they nevertheless were ingredients of a scheme which *as a whole* affected interstate commerce and hence fell within Congress' regulatory and protective powers.

Commenting on this case eighteen years later, Chief Justice Taft justly remarked:

That case was a milestone in the interpretation of the "commerce clause" of the Constitution. It recognized the great changes and development in the business of this vast country and drew again the dividing line between interstate and intrastate commerce where the Constitution had intended it to be. It refused to permit local incidents of a great interstate movement, which taken alone were intrastate, to characterize the movement as such.[83]

The decision, indeed, not only pumped restorative blood into the collapsed Sherman Act; its reviving effect presently reached Congress itself, with the result that in 1921 and 1922 that body enacted the Packers and Stockyards Act and the Grain Futures Act, the former of which places the business of livestock dealers and commission men in the principal stockyards of the country under national supervision, while the latter imposes a similar control upon the buying and selling of grain on boards of trade and through other exchanges or associations.

Speaking for the Court in *Stafford* v. *Wallace*,[84] which involved the Stockyards Act, Chief Justice Taft said:

The object to be secured by the act is the free and unburdened flow of livestock from the ranges and farms of the West and Southwest through the great stockyards and slaughtering centers on the borders of that region, and thence in the form of meat products to the consuming cities of the country in the Middle West and East, or, still as livestock, to the feeding places and fattening farms in the Middle West or East for further preparation for the market. The chief evil feared is the monopoly of the packers, enabling them unduly and arbitrarily to lower prices to the shipper who sells, and unduly and arbitrarily to increase the price to the consumer who buys.

But there were other evils, too, against which the act was aimed: exorbitant charges, duplication of commissions, deceptive practices, and so on and so forth; for if charges be "unreasonable, they are an undue burden on the commerce which the stockyards are intended to facilitate. . . . The stockyards are not a place of rest or final destination," they "are but a throat through which the current flows." The sales there

are not in this aspect merely local transactions. . . . They merely change the private interests in the subject of the current, not interfering with, but, on the contrary, being indispensable to its continuity. The origin of the livestock is in the West, its ultimate destination known to, and intended by, all engaged in the business is in the Middle West and East, either as meat products or stock for feeding and fattening. This is the definite and understood course of business. The stockyards and the sales are necessary factors in the middle of this current of commerce.[85]

This is a striking description of what interstate

commerce in a particular product has today become; and is a striking authentication of the fact that the business in question is today dominated by its interstate characteristics. What we are called upon to vision is a current which has its source in certain acts, or procedures, of production; which takes its way across the country with ever increasing volume and without interruption by, or even awareness of, state lines; which comes to pause now and again in an eddy, as it were, for certain further operations and transactions, including again acts of production (the preparation of meat products, fattening on the farms), but which ever resumes its flow to its diverse and nation-spread destination in what may be termed *the national market*.

And what is said here of the meat business may with equal truth be said of half a hundred other species of traffic—in California's fruit, in Minnesota's flour, in Texas' oil, in Pennsylvania's coal, in Kentucky's tobacco, in Michigan's automobiles, etc. Business, in short, is today a *continuum*, in which its local phases have become submerged; "in this aspect," to use Chief Justice Taft's words, they cease being merely local. Nor is there any other term for this *continuum* but "interstate commerce," since it exists for, and is altogether dependent upon, the interstate, the *national market*. And it is in the light of this fact that Congress' protective power over interestate commerce must today be evaluated, inasmuch as the health of the part is inevitably a function of the health of the

whole. More than that, however, the health of
any particular line of business is a function of the
health of business as a whole, of the entire economic and industrial organism.

Nor does "Nira" necessarily do more than assert
this. Madamoiselle is not inarticulate. She delivers
her *apologia pro sua vita* in the following words:

A national emergency productive of widespread unemployment and disorganization of industry, which burdens
interstate and foreign commerce, affects the public welfare, and undermines the standards of living of the
American people, is hereby declared to exist. It is hereby
declared to be the policy of Congress to remove obstructions to the free flow of interstate and foreign commerce
which tend to diminish the amount thereof; and to provide for the general welfare by promoting the organization of industry for the purpose of cooperative action
among trade groups, to induce and maintain united action
of labor and management under adequate governmental
sanctions and supervision, to eliminate unfair competitive
practices, to promote the fullest possible utilization of
the present productive capacity of industries, to avoid
undue restriction of production (except as may be tem-
porarily required), to increase the consumption of industrial and agricultural products by increasing purchasing
power, to reduce and relieve unemployment, to improve
standards of labor, and otherwise to rehabilitate industry
and to conserve national resources.[86]

That the present Court will regard this plea
sympathetically appears today not at all unlikely.
At least it has already blazed a fairly feasible trail
to such a consummation, even though not every

difficulty has as yet been removed therefrom. The words of the Chief Justice in the Appalachian Coals Case, decided shortly before Nira was enacted, were undoubtedly before its authors: "When industry is grievously hurt, when producing concerns fail, when unemployment mounts, and communities dependent upon profitable production are prostrate, the wells of commerce go dry."[87] Witness, too, the Chief Justice's opinion for the Court in the Minnesota Moratorium Case, with its invocation of Marshall's doctrine of adaptative interpretation, and its insistence upon change in *outlook* as something which must be taken into account, no less than change in *conditions*, if the Constitution is to be kept viable;[88] and the implications of the decision in the New York Milk Case[89] are no less auspicious.

It will be urged no doubt that, considered as typifying or foreshadowing a permanent system of legislation, Nira spells the end, or at least the complete subordination, of state power over business and industry, and hence the end of the dual federal principle within this predominantly important field of governmental action. Nor do I see how this assertion can be gainsaid. But the simple and sufficient answer is that in so doing the act merely sounds the knell of a departed day, and for the reason stated by Professor Gulick in his address at Chicago last summer: *"Nothing effective can be done in the regulation or stabilization of economic affairs unless the area of planning and control has the same boundaries as the economic structure.*"[90]

In other words, the only way to restore dual federalism as a viable method of political control in the field of industry would be to break up the industrial structure. Otherwise, except for control by the national government, only one alternative remains, and that is the restoration of the system under which the present situation developed, the system whose beneficiaries cried up state power when they wished to check national power and cried up national power when they wished to check state power—whose dominating conception of constitutional law has all along been that of a set of devices enabling them to play both ends against the middle and thereby escape all governmental supervision.[91]

I hardly need to point out that the question of the viability in modern conditions of the notion of dual federalism has other aspects than the one particularly discussed in the preceding pages. Not only has state power broken down in the sphere of business regulation; it has also broken down in that most ancient of governmental spheres, the prevention and repression of crimes of violence. Nor has this been due merely or largely to corrupt or incompetent administration in the state and local governments, although that has doubtless been at times a contributing cause. Yet the principal factor, manifestly, has been the vast development in recent decades of the facilities of interstate intercourse—commerce in Marshall's sense; and quite appropriately, therefore, the national government has proceeded farther and farther into the field of criminal legislation along the route of the "commerce" clause.[92] The validity of such legislation is no longer seriously challenged; any more than is that type of legislation which is styled "federal grants in aid," whereby through its fiscal powers the national government has come to direct to an important extent the rendition of social services by the local governments. The matter will be touched upon again in a later chapter. All in all, dual federalism is today in serious case.

To sum up: From the *Federalist* itself issue the first beginnings of two divergent theories of national power, the contributions of Hamilton and Madison, respectively. By the Hamiltonian theory, the national government, although a government of enumerated powers, is within the range of these powers a truly sovereign government, and so is under no constitutional compulsion, either in the selection of means whereby to make its powers effective or in the selection of objects to be attained by their exercise, to take account of the coexistence of the states or to concern itself to preserve any particular relationship of power between itself and the states. And this also was the theory of the men who "put across" the Constitution and who set the national government going. Also it is the theory which underlies Chief Justice Marshall's famous decisions.

For all that, the outlook embodied in the theory was not that of the great mass of the American people either in 1789 or even three quarters of a century later. Their experience was local, their immediate interest local, and through Jefferson and Madison this localistic outlook found expression in a far different version of the Constitution, one which treated it as resulting primarily from a compact among the states and which required that its interpretation be directed to the preservation in the states of their accustomed powers and to the maintenance of that greatest of constitutional contrivances, dual federalism. And in fact the constitutional jurisprudence of the Court conformed largely to these objectives for a full half century succeeding Marshall's death, save as it made accommodation for the more evident lessons of the Civil War.

It resulted that by the year 1885 the Court found itself able in all cases raising the question of national power to choose between two well matured but sharply divergent traditions. At the same moment it began to be played upon by two sometimes conflicting, sometimes accordant influences emanating from the realm of economic thought and activity. One of these was the growing popular awareness of the national basis of prosperity; the other was that mode of thinking concerning the relationship of government and business which goes by the name of *laissez faire*—a compound of the teachings of the Manchester school of political economy and a highly sentimentalized version of the doctrine of evolution. From these sources, separately or in combination, the deduction was drawn—in university circles especially—that society had only to permit its more impudent and hard-boiled members to indulge their acquisitive faculties to the top of their bent, and a millennium would presently dawn for all. And enjoying such excellent chaperonage, this belief came inevitably to impress the "naif, simple-minded men" who made up the Court of that day, while, by an equal inevitability, they proceeded to spin from it a new constitutional law.

The chief power of the national government enabling it to interpose in the field of economic activity has been in the past that which it derives from the "commerce" clause. Beginning about 1885 the Court's construction of this clause underwent a curious development, largely in response to the *laissez faire* impulse. Applied as a restriction to state power, the terms of the clause were given a liberal interpretation which became a material factor in furthering the reorganization of American business on a national scale and its attendant subjection to a highly concentrated management. Applied, on the other hand, as a grant of national power, these same terms suffered a marked contraction from the doctrines of Chief Justice Marshall, "commerce" being confined to *transportation* mainly, and the power to "regulate" it being conceived as chiefly a power to *protect* and *promote* it by the adoption of measures beneficial to it when regarded as a purely private enterprise.

This type of constitutional law is today at an end. Under modern conditions commerce is not, if it ever was, a purely private enterprise, and its protection and promotion unavoidably exact the use of judgment as to what is good in the long run both for commerce and for the community. Nor does the concept of dual federalism correspond to the actualities of commerce and industry today, a fact which the Court under the leadership of Justices Holmes, Hughes, and Taft has increasingly recognized. The Shreveport Case brusquely dismissed dual federalism as having no longer any pertinence to the question of railway rate legislation. This was in 1914. But already a decade earlier, Holmes's opinion in the Swift Case had laid down the guiding lines toward a similar result in the field of business regulation generally, lines which were emphasized and extended in Chief Justice Taft's opinions in 1922.

And Nira purports to build upon these results, extending them in response to the lessons of the depression. It posits the solidarity of American economic life, the interdependence of all its phases, and it proffers a conception of unfair methods of competition which is a necessary deduction from this solidarity and interdependence. In some respects Nira is a revolutionary statute, yet the revolution which it embodies is only the legal counterpart of a revolution already accomplished by science, invention, and business management in the field of commerce and industry, and represents an effort—not necessarily the best conceived effort—

to give established economic trends a socially beneficial direction.

In the pregnant words of the Court, "Primitive
conditions have passed; business is now transacted
on a national scale";[93] and, it may be added, so is
crime. For which reasons, as well as others, while
invocation of the doctrine of dual federalism may
still be pardonable as a gesture of farewell to an
era that will return no more, it is certainly of
limited helpfulness in solving the problem of fit-
ting our constitutional system to present-day
needs. As between the thesis of dual federalism and
that of nationalism ineluctable forces have chosen.
We should, perhaps, congratulate ourselves that
the resources of our constitutional law and theory
afford us choices which put it into our power to go
far without a more obvious breach with our institutional past.[94]

CHAPTER II

THE PROPERTY RIGHT VERSUS LEGISLATIVE POWER IN A DEMOCRACY

I.

THE Constitution of the United States has been frequently stigmatized "a reactionary document," but the characterization requires explanation if it is to be accurately understood. Actually, all things considered, the hospitality manifested in the Constitution to the rising forces of *political* democracy is not a little surprising. The state legislatures, whose malignant courses affecting rights of creditors and similar interests had been a principal cause of the Convention,[1] were still left vast powers, and in addition were wrought directly into the new structure, as in the choice of senators and presidential electors. Likewise the Convention voted down every motion looking to the imposition of property qualifications for the suffrage or for office-holding, not necessarily because its members disapproved of such expedients, but because they saw no prospect of getting them accepted. The question of suffrage, in fact, was ultimately relegated to the states themselves, with the result that the development of democracy in the new system was made dependent on its farther advance in the states, where it was conceded already to be "excessive." The attitude taken toward the rising West was similarly pragmatic. Gouverneur Morris, asserting that "the busy haunts of men, and not the remote wilderness, was the proper school of political talents," demanded that the new states to be admitted from the West should be subjected to a rule of representation that would still leave the East in the ascendancy;[2] but all such efforts were rejected in favor of the principle of equal treatment. In a word, the Convention recognized that the doctrines of the political equality of men and of political democracy had become, for better or for worse, fixed data of the American constitutional system, and that any attempt to combat this fact would only invite defeat.

On the other hand, that the Convention never for a moment relinquished the intention which it cherished from the outset of utilizing the new system for the purpose of throwing special safeguards about proprietarian interests, is equally apparent. In Article I, Section 10, of the Constitution certain restraints were laid upon the states for the protection particularly of creditors. "No state," the clause runs, "shall . . . emit bills of credit, make anything but gold or silver coin a tender in payment of debts, pass any bill of attainder, *ex post facto* law or law impairing the obligation of contracts."

And in constituting the Supreme Court the Convention endowed it with attributes which, while removing that body from contaminating touch with the daily aberrations of public opinion, were ingeniously calculated to foster among its members a corporate spirit, a sense of calling, *an instinct for power*. The Court is small, the cream (sometimes not very fat cream) of a profession in which the political impulse is strong; its members hold office during good behavior, and are assured, so long as the currency is not unduly inflated, of a comfortable livelihood. Its deliberations are in private—one might well say, in secret; and its determinations were commonly thought in an age when the doctrine of natural law was a universal tenet, to be invested with the impersonality of fate itself.

Finally the Convention, in a spirit of truly audacious experimentation, tied Article I, Section 10, to the Supreme Court by means of judicial review. The notion of judicial review had, to be sure, already been broached in several of the states, but it was not a working institution in a single one of them.[3] Its tentative beginnings had shown, nevertheless, and the Convention took alert notice of the fact, that the general leanings of the state judiciaries were vastly more conservative than were those of the state assemblies, vastly more tender of proprietarian interests.

Hamilton's classic essay in *Federalist 78* testifies to the current speculations. Judicial review, he there asserted, would not be confined simply to the task of preserving the *written* Constitution from infractions. Independent judges would also be in position to mitigate laws which extended "no further than to the injury of *particular classes*," and indeed to check the legislative body "in passing them." This, he added, was "a circumstance calculated to have more influence upon the character of our governments than but few may be aware of. The benefits of the integrity and moderation of the judiciary have already been felt in more states than one."[4]

The formative period of American constitutional law reaches, roughly speaking, to 1830. Its outstanding characteristic is the persistence in the courts, *state as well as national,* of the ideas which had swayed the Convention of 1787 and had subsequently furnished the creed of the Federalist party. And with one exception the outstanding contributions of the period to American constitutional law and theory, reflecting this harmonizing influence, were *the joint enterprise of the national and state judiciaries.* Marshall's doctrines of national power were not of his own creation, but their assimilation into our constitutional jurisprudence was his personal achievement. The doctrine of judicial review, on the other hand, the supporting doctrine that the authority to construe the standing law with finality is "judicial" and not "legislative," and what for convenience' sake may be termed the Doctrine of Vested Rights—our present concern—are all fruits of this unique coöperation. With good reason did De Tocqueville, writing at the close of this period, remark: "If I were asked where I placed the American aristocracy, I should reply without hesitation that it is not composed of the rich, who are not united together by any common tie, but that it occupies the judicial bench and the bar."[5]

Albeit enforced with varying degrees of rigor in different jurisdictions, *the doctrine of vested rights*[6] is sufficiently described as a notification by the courts that they would disallow any legislative act which they found to bear unduly harshly upon existing property rights, or else would construe the act in such a way as to avoid this effect. And as the application of the doctrine varied in the different jurisdictions, so was it supported by a variety of arguments. At the outset the doctrine owed much to the current deism, which was complacently wont to refer all existing arrangements to a beneficent divine intention; and coöperating with this factor was another, that lack of clear distinction between the ethical and the strictly legal which a prevalence of "higher law" concepts usually betokens. Property, it was urged, was of transcendental origin, having been instituted among men in furtherance of their social and moral improvement, and it was protected by natural law, the principles of the social compact, and the principles of republican government.[7] But even stronger support was eventually lent by the effort which the wish to provide a secure logical basis for judicial review stimulated, to define "legislative power" in relation to "judicial power." The former, it was posited, was only the power to make *new* law, while the determination of rights under the *standing* law was exclusively the province of courts; and a legislative act interfering with existing rights of ownership, especially those of named parties, was such a determination of rights adversely, and hence tantamount to "a bill of pains and penalties," however commendable may have been the motives of the legislative body in passing it.[8]

There was a time when the doctrine, and particularly the aspect of it just mentioned, seemed likely to find lodgment in the prohibition on "*ex post facto* laws" of the national Constitution. That some at least of the framers designed this clause for the very purpose of putting a stop to the legislative practice common in many of the states in 1787, of interfering with the decisions of the ordinary courts affecting rights of property and contract, there can be little question.[9] In the early case of *Calder* v. *Bull*,[10] however, this hope was frustrated by a decision confining the clause to penal legislation. The Court was still feeble and by no means certain of its rôle, and the outcome of the broader construction, said Justice Chase, "could not be foreseen." Yet at the same time, he endeavored to assuage the disappointment which the Court was fully aware its decision would produce, by assailing vigorously the notion of legislative "omnipotence" and by pointing to transcendental principles protective of the property right, which, he insinuated, could be properly enforced by the state courts if they but chose to essay the task.

The elaboration of the doctrine of vested rights accordingly now passed to the state judiciaries in the main, assisted, nevertheless, by the national

courts in cases which fell to their jurisdiction because of the diverse citizenship of the parties, and
where the law to be applied was theoretically state
law. Such a case, for instance, and one which in the
sequel proved to be of immense importance, was
Fletcher v. *Peck*,[11] in which Marshall, in 1810,
pronounced void an act of the Georgia legislature
rescinding a previous grant of land by the same
body, on the ground that such a measure did not
fall within "legislative power," was contrary to the
"spirit of our institutions," and violated the "obligation of contracts" clause of the national Constitution. In the Dartmouth College Case[12] a decade
later, the benefit of this last proposition was
extended to corporate charters. That entire body
of constitutional law whereby the Court extended
to *public grants* a protection which was intended
for *private executory contracts* only, was originally but a rib from the side of the broader doctrine of vested rights.

By 1830 the doctrine of vested rights had come
to be accepted in the great majority of the states
of the Union, perhaps in all of them; while the list
of judges who had had a hand in bringing this result about is a most impressive one: Marshall, Wilson, Paterson, Story, Johnson, Kent, Walworth,
Grimke, Parsons, Hosmer, Ruffin, Buchanan, and
others. Indeed, he would have been a bold man who
at this date would have ventured to challenge the
"higher law" presuppositions of the doctrine, as is
shown by the circumstances which surrounded the
argument and decision of the case of *Wilkinson* v.

Leland[13] by the Supreme Court in 1829. The attorney of defendants in error was Daniel Webster.
"If," said he, "at this period, there is not a general restraint on legislatures, in favor of private
rights, there is an end to private property.
Though there may be no prohibition in the constitution, the legislature is restrained from acts sub-
verting the great principles of republican liberty
and of the social compact." To this contention his
opponent, William Wirt, responded thus: "Who is
the sovereign? Is it not the legislature of the state
and are not its acts effectual, unless they come in
contact with the great principles of the social compact?" The act of the Rhode Island legislature under review was upheld, but said Justice Story,
speaking for the Court: "That government can
scarcely be deemed to be free where the rights of
property are left solely dependent upon the will of
a legislative body without any restraint. The fundamental maxims of a free government seem to require that the rights of personal liberty and private property should be held sacred."

But unquestionably the name which is associated preëminently with the final embodiment of
the vested rights principle in American constitutional law is that of Chancellor Kent. Indeed, his
contribution was manifold and pervasive. Its start-
ing-point is a particular construction of the Cok-
ian maxim (which traces back, *via* Bracton, to the
Justinian Code): "*Nova constitutio futuris formam imponere debet non praeteritis;* a new law
should apply to future matters and not to things

past."[14] Invoking this maxim, Kent concurred in
holding in the case of *Dash* v. *Van Kleeck*,[15] decided in 1811, that a statute which in sweeping
terms had abolished a certain right of action by
creditors was inapplicable to an action brought before the statute's enactment. His opinion in the
case is doubly creative. In the first place, it infers
that any law which takes away a *property* right
(which is what he held the right of action involved
in the case to be) is for that reason *retroactive*
within the sense of the maxim, although originally
this was certainly not so.[16] Secondly, it transforms
what had been heretofore a simple principle of
statutory construction into one of compulsive constitutional obligation: courts must never apply
general statutes in such a way as to destroy *vested
rights*—a doctrine which Kent endeavors to bol-
ster by references to writers on the Law of Nature
and Nations, to the principle of the Separation of
Powers, and—most astonishingly—to the term
"due process of law."[17] More than a generation
later the New York courts, after first setting aside
the then recently enacted Married Women's Property Act, reconsidered the question, and applying
Kent's doctrine to the measure, sustained it as regards *future* acquisitions by wives[18]—thus afford-
ing, it may be noted in passing, an excellent illustration of Hamilton's suggestion in *Federalist 78*,
of judicial review by *construction*, as well as by
outright disallowance.

Furthermore, in his famous *Commentaries* Kent
set forth a systematic theory of the powers of gov-

ernment in the United States in which these were
carefully "treated"—in the chemical sense—with
the vested rights principle. The power of eminent
domain was the power to take property for what
should be *judicially* found to be a "public purpose," after compensation should have been rendered both for the property actually taken and for
that substantially injured. The power of taxation
was likewise restricted to "public purposes," inasmuch as it was only as a member of the public that
the taxpayer could retrieve his *quid pro quo;* and
taxes must be levied by the rule of proportion.
Lastly, the state had also the power to "prescribe
the mode and manner of using it [property], so
far as may be necessary to prevent the abuse of the
right to the injury or annoyance of others or of
the public." This, however, was not, Kent makes it
amply clear, a power to destroy property values in
the hands of owners without paying them, and it
was not a power "to limit the extent of the acquisition of property." "A state of equality as to property," he wrote in his lecture on "The History,
Progress and Absolute Rights of Property," "is
impossible to be maintained, for it is against the
laws of our own nature; and if it could be reduced
to practice, it would place the human race in a
state of tasteless enjoyment and stupid inactivity,
which would degrade the mind and destroy the
happiness of social life;" while by the same token,
civil government was not entitled, "in ordinary
cases, . . . to regulate the uses of property in the
hands of the owners by sumptuary laws or any

other visionary schemes of frugality and equality.
. . . No such fatal union (as some have supposed) necessarily exists between prosperity and
tyranny or between wealth and national corruption in the harmonious arrangements of Providence." *Liberty* "*depends essentially upon the
structure of government,* the administration of
justice and the intelligence of the people, and it
has very little concern with equality of property
and frugality of living. . . ."[19]

II.

THE question arises of the relation of the doctrine
of vested rights to the ever increasing forces of political democracy in the United States. The doctrine was of course but an aspect—or perhaps one
should say, the residuum—of the much broader
proposal in 1787 to give property a special position in the constitutional system, and the harmony
of such an idea with American social conditions
was debated on the floor of the Philadelphia Convention itself. There the younger Pinckney had
opposed a suggestion to make the Senate representative of property on the ground that, in view
of the general equality of condition of the American population, the proposal was pointless. What
was more, he asserted, in words curiously pro-
phetic of the century to follow, though their vati-
cination is now spent, this condition was bound to
continue. "In a new country," said he, "possessing
immense tracts of uncultivated lands, where every

temptation is offered to emigration, and where industry must be rewarded with competency, there will be few poor and fewer dependent."[20]

Madison, on the other hand, had dissented both from Pinckney's description of existing conditions and from his forecast of the future. He declared:

We cannot be regarded, even at this time, as one homogeneous mass, in which everything that affects a part will in the same manner affect the whole, . . . [while] in framing a system which we wish to last for ages, we should not lose sight of the changes which ages will produce. An increase of population will of necessity increase the proportion of those who will labor under all the hardships of life, and secretly sigh for a more equal distribution of its blessings. . . . How is this danger to be guarded against on republican principles? . . . Among other means, by the establishment of a body in the government, sufficiently respectable for its wisdom and virtue to aid, on such emergencies, the preponderance of justice, by throwing its weight into that scale.[21]

The proposal to base representation in the Senate on property fell through, but as we have seen, "the respectable body" was provided from another quarter.

And the divergence of outlook which is thus illustrated reappears later even among the supporters of the vested rights principle. Kent's tone, as appears from the passage quoted above from his *Commentaries*, was very high; and it would hardly be venturesome to conjecture that he shared the view of such Federalists as Hamilton and the elder Adams, that inequalities in wealth were the natu-

ral and desirable fruitage of liberal institutions.[22]
The attitude of Webster, on the other hand, as expressed in the Massachusetts Convention of 1820
was very different. While arguing strongly that it
was "the part of political wisdom to found government on property," he accompanied this observation with the declaration that "the freest government, if it could exist, would not long be accept-
able, if the tendency of the laws were to create a
rapid accumulation of property in few hands, and
to render the great mass of the population dependent and penniless." Nor, he continued, was this the
tendency of "our laws":

With property divided, as we have it, no other government
than that of a republic could be maintained. . . . There
is reason, therefore, to expect a long continuance of our
systems. Party and passion, doubtless may prevail at
times, and much temporary damage be done. . . . But a
great revolution in regard to property must take place
before our governments can be moved from their republican basis.[23]

In short, the doctrine of vested rights was welcomed by some as a constitutional bulwark of potential aristocracy, while by others it was defended
as a device of democracy itself for the protection
of a right shared by all with substantial equality,
against the casual injustices of democratic government. At the same time, the actual tendency of the
doctrine as a principle of *constitutional law* was
quite unambiguous. This was, in brief, to crystal-
lize the ordinary law affecting property rights, or

in other words, to sterilize legislative power in respect of such rights. Yet, in fact, this tendency
was finally averted—how? The answer is to be
found in the Doctrine of the Police Power, the rise
of which presents us in relation to the doctrine of
vested rights the second of the great antinomies of
American constitutional theory with which we have
to deal in these pages.

The term "police power" seems to have made its
début into the vocabulary of American constitutional law in 1827 in Marshall's opinion on *Brown*
v. *Maryland*.[24] Here it designates the residual
powers of the state legislatures, minus those of
taxation and eminent domain—what Kent had
termed the "power of regulation." The *doctrine of
the police power* is something very different, something very much more—it is the police power
grown up and fortunately wedded to a new point
of view in constitutional law. By the doctrine of
vested rights all legislative programs stood or fell
by the single test of their operation upon private
rights having cash value. By the doctrine of the
police power the *public welfare* was for the first
time erected into a *judicially cognizable* justification of legislative activity, even when it touched
property rights.[25]

Classic expression was given the new point of
view in 1837 in Chief Justice Taney's opinion in
the Charles River Bridge Case,[26] where the doctrine of strict construction of charter grants was
laid down. "The object and end of all government," the opinion runs, "is to promote the happi-

ness and prosperity of the community by which it was established; and it can never be assumed that the government intended to diminish its power of accomplishing the end for which it was created."[27] Even earlier, the Court had given notification that it would henceforth protect no vested rights except those clearly covered by the "obligation of contracts" clause—a pledge consistently observed until after the Civil War.[28]

These and other decisions of like tenor in both the national and local jurisdictions proved stimulative. In the years following occurred a fresh release of legislative energies comparable to that in the early days of the War of Independence. The Thirties saw the firm establishment of the public-school system, the Forties witnessed the elimination of coverture from the common law, in the Fifties the first wave of antiliquor legislation swept over parts of the country. Then came the period divided by the Civil War, when the Supreme Court itself, merging the doctrine of the police power with the principle of state sovereignty, talked at times as if the amalgam was entitled to override all constitutional limitations, and the "obligation of contracts" clause was for the time being almost obliterated from the Constitution. In *Dix* v. *West River Bridge*,[29] decided in 1848, the Court ruled that all public grants were subject to the state's inherent and inalienable power of eminent domain; and a quarter century later kindred doctrine was laid down as to the police power, in relation to public health, safety, and morals.[30] Today the protection afforded by the "obligation of contracts" clause has been to a great extent absorbed into that general principle of judicial discretion wherein all constitutional restraints have tended latterly to lose identity.[31]

But if the developing concept of the police power affected the standing of the doctrine of vested rights, still more did the broader principle of which this concept was but a phase. I mean the principle of Popular Sovereignty, of which Jackson was at once chief symbol and hierophant. "The people rule" was the simple Jacksonian gospel; and from this point of view the state constitution, even the parts of it intended for the protection of individual rights, assumed a new coloration. Ceasing to be considered declaratory of transcendental law, it claimed obedience as expressing the will of the people—as the enactment, in short, of sovereign law-making authority. This being so, however, what were the courts to do with the doctrine of vested rights? There were two choices open to them and only two; they must discard the doctrine, or they must cast about it some phrase of the *written* constitution, that supreme emanation from popular *will*.

From this dilemma there initially resulted, in the Forties and Fifties, a number of makeshift doctrines—though several of them were destined to survive the period—the *raison d'être* of which was to preserve the benefits of the vested rights principle against the rising tide of democratic self-assertion. Kent's doctrine of "public purpose"

spread to other jurisdictions.[32] The maxim that
the "legislature cannot delegate its power" was
called into service against the earliest forms of
antiliquor legislation, local option laws.[33] In
Massachusetts the phrase "reasonable legislation"
from the state constitution was brought under
judicial construction, thus prefiguring one of the
most important developments of modern constitutional law.[34] Here also Chief Justice Shaw for the
first time associated the police power with the Cok-
ian maxim, "*sic utere tuo ut alienum non laedas*,"[35]
whereby the police power was later on put into
leading strings to the common law, more particularly the law of nuisance.[36] Meantime, in North
Carolina an earlier suggestion that the term "law
of the land" in that state's constitution meant
"general law" and hence ruled out special legislative acts determinative of private rights,[37] had
been expanded into a ratification of Kent's
broader doctrine that even general statutes might
not be validly applied "retrospectively," that is to
say, detrimentally to acquisitions under previous
law.[38] And building on this result the New York
courts between the later Thirties and the early
Fifties finally succeeded in bringing the doctrine
of vested rights within the shelter of the "due
process of law" clause of that state's constitution.[39]
Thus this singular quest of a constitutional limitation for a constitutional provision happily attained its goal at last!

To the lay mind the term "due process of law"

suggests at once a form of trial, with the result that if it limits the legislature at all, it is only when that body is delineating the *process* whereby the legislative will is to be *applied* to specific cases; and a little research soon demonstrates that the lay mind is probably right so far as the history of the matter is concerned.[40] How, then, came this clause to furnish basis for the challenge by a defendant to the validity of the rule under which he is called to account? The initial step was Kent's definition of "due process of law" as *judicial process*.[41] The inference intended is that, in conformity with the "due process" clause, no one may be actually *deprived* of property except by judicial process, which means, of course, by judicial application of the *standing* law, since to apply the standing law is the judicial function and all of it. "Due process of law" means, therefore, the standing law; *therefore, the law under which the property was acquired.*

Unfortunately the demonstration does not demonstrate, for the reason that the vital question is begged. This is, why should the "standing law," to which the judicial power is admittedly obliged to lend enforcement, be considered as *excluding* a freshly enacted statute whose *judicial enforcement* —that is, by definition, enforcement by "due process"—would *deprive* a person of property? The only reply forthcoming is, just because it would do this. In other words, *the term "due process of law" simply drops out of the constitutional clause when*

way is made in it for the doctrine of vested rights;
and, it may be added, the words "life" and "liberty" do likewise.

And a second argument, often made or inferred in behalf of the above application of the "due process" clause, is open to the same criticism. This argument invokes Chief Justice Marshall's dictum in *Brown* v. *Maryland*, that constitutional restraints look not to "form" but to "substance."[42] The suggestion is that "due process of law" is the *form*, the property right the *substance*.[43] Once again, therefore, the protection of the clause is treated as absolute, once again this absolute protection is confined to the property right.

The absorption of the doctrine of vested rights into the "due process" clause of the New York constitution was perfected in 1856 by the decision of the Court of Appeals in the famous Wynehamer Case,[44] where a state-wide antiliquor act was invalidated on the ground that as to existing stocks of liquor it constituted an act of deprivation not within the power of government to perform "*even by the forms which belong to due process of law.*"[45] Contemporaneously several other state courts were deciding similar issues in precisely the opposite way, and invoking the police power in justification.[46] So, as the Civil War was about to break, the ancient conundrum, what happens when an irresistible force encounters an immovable body, was reincarnated as a problem of constitutional interpretation—Who was to solve it?

III.

SOLUTION was, in fact, postponed by the war; then facilitated by its outcome. In the year 1868 occurred two events which render that date a pivotal one in the history of American constitutional law. I refer to the adoption of the Fourteenth Amendment and the publication of Cooley's *Constitutional Limitations*. Chapter XI of this celebrated work, bearing the title "Protection to Property by 'Law of the Land,' " is a compendium of state decisions prior to 1868, asserting and illustrating the doctrine of vested rights; while Chapter XVI, bearing the title "The Police Power of the States," performs a comparable service for the rival doctrine. Thus was the national Supreme Court on the one hand invested with a new jurisdiction of untested potentialities over state legislative power, and, on the other hand, supplied with a double set of answers, each duly authenticated by supporting precedents, to all questions capable of arising within this jurisdiction and touching the vital problem of the relation of legislative power to the property right.

Nevertheless, the Court seems at first to have been genuinely reluctant to enter upon its new legacy of power. For one thing, it was afraid that if it made a liberal interpretation of the terms of section 1 of the amendment, Congress would be the organ of the national government to be aggrandized, in consequence of its powers of "appropriate legislation" under the fifth section of the amendment. In the Slaughter House Cases,[47] protesting that it had no ambition to become a "perpetual censor upon all legislation of the states," and exalting the police power mightily, the Court virtually erased the "privileges and immunities" clause from the amendment in deference to the federal principle. But its action was against the strenuous protest of four members, and in one of the opinions filed by the dissenters, that of Justice Bradley, the attention of the Bar was directed to the speculative possibilities of the "due process of law" clause and especially of the word "liberty" thereof.[48] The decision in *Munn* v. *Illinois*,[49] four years later, is also perceived today to have been an equivocal triumph for the police power. The Court sustained the right of a state legislature to set finally and conclusively the "charges" of "businesses affected with a public interest," but on the basis of an opinion by the Chief Justice which is easily interpretable as restricting the police power to the mere work of implementing the common law. Indeed, as is pointed out below, the Court has come long since to exercise in this field too a power of review of indefinite scope.

But in 1876 this development was as yet a long way off; the Court was still fighting fate even while inviting it. In *Davidson* v. *New Orleans*,[50] the year following the Munn decision, Justice Miller rated the lawyers soundly for crowding the docket of the Court with cases in which it was "asked to hold that state legislatures had deprived

their own citizens of life, liberty or property without 'due process of law.' " "There is here," he continued, "abundant evidence that there exists some
strange misconception of the scope of the provision." Yet he himself declined to supplement ad-
monition with instruction. "There is wisdom, we
think," said he, "in the ascertaining of the intent
and application of such an important phrase in the
Federal Constitution, by the gradual process of
judicial inclusion and exclusion, as the cases . . .
shall require."[51]

"Virtue is its own reward," and none more certainly than that which knows how to face both
ways. The pressure upon the Court to become a
third house of every legislature in the country
waxed constantly stronger. The owners of the rail-
roads of the country were now largely Easterners,
and Chief Justice Waite's counsel in the Munn
Case "to go to the polls and not the courts"[52] was
colder comfort than ever. Industrial consolidation
was also getting under way to the tune of *laissez
faire* and economic individualism.[53] Nor did fear
of what Congress might do under the fifth section
of the amendment longer weigh upon the Court,
thanks to the fact that the Democrats were now
in control of the House of Representatives once
more, to say nothing of the further fact that the
decision in the Civil Rights Cases[54] had pretty well
emasculated the section anyway.

In deciding the case of *Hurtado* v. *California*[55]
in 1884, the Court at last made a definite gesture
of acceptance toward the crown it had heretofore

repulsed. Plaintiff in error, who had received sentence of death for murder, urged that the proceedings against him lacked due process since they had not included indictment by grand jury. Inasmuch as Coke in his *Institutes* defines "due process of law" precisely as "indictment or presentment of good and lawful men . . . or by writ original of the common law," it is apparent that Hurtado's contention was, so far as history alone is concerned, rather strongly grounded. The Court ruled, nevertheless, that the "due process" clause of Amendment XIV left the states unhampered by the common law in improving their modes of trial, so long as these continued fair and just; but along with the ruling went the warning that the clause was intended to make the "fundamental principles of liberty and justice" an always available test *through judicial review of state power in all of its branches.* Justice Mathews said:

The limitations imposed by our constitutional law (*sic.*) upon the action of the governments, both state and national, are essential to the preservation of public and private rights, notwithstanding the representative character of our political institutions. The enforcement of these limitations by judicial process is the device of self-governing communities to protect the rights of individuals and minorities . . . against the power of numbers.[56]

Or more compactly expressed, *due process of law* meant *constitutional law*, that is, at that date, *state constitutional law*, that is, Cooley's *Constitu-*

tional Limitations. But did it mean more particularly Chapter XI of that work or Chapter XVI?

At this point chance became an accelerating factor in developments. In volume 111 *United States Reports,* through circumstances that need not be detailed here, Justice Bradley was enabled to repeat the substance of his dissent in the Slaughter House Cases as the opinion of a *concurring* minority;[57] and forthwith certain of the state courts deemed themselves authorized to treat the views thus reiterated as those of the Court itself.[58] Two years later Senator Roscoe Conkling, a former member of the famous Joint Committee on Reconstruction, in which the Fourteenth Amendment was framed, introduced in argument before the Court certain passages from the committee's Journal with the purpose of showing that the protection of the amendment against discriminatory state legislation had been by no means intended solely for the new class of Freedmen—as Justice Miller had declared in the Slaughter House Cases —but had been meant to embrace all "persons," corporations included, in all their rights.[59] It is true, of course, that even as early as *Munn* v. *Illinois,* the Court had virtually indicated that the protection of the amendment could be invoked by proprietarian interests and by corporations. Yet that Conkling's argument had some effect may be inferred from the Chief Justice's opinion shortly following it in the Railroad Commission Cases, in which he gave warning that the power of rate regulation was "not a . . . power of confiscation";[60] and also by the Court's decision a year later in *Yick Wo* v. *Hopkins*,[61] where the protection of the amendment was held to embrace every class and condition of mankind.

Then in 1887 the Court was confronted in *Mugler* v. *Kansas*[62] with a state-wide Prohibition law of the very kind that had been overruled thirty years before by the New York Court of Appeals in the Wynehamer Case. Speaking for the Court, Justice Harlan phrased the issue as follows: It belongs with the state legislature, in exercise of the police powers of the state, "to determine, primarily, what measures are appropriate or needful for the protection of the public morals, the public health, or the public safety." However,

if . . . a statute purporting to have been enacted to protect the public health, the public morals, or the public safety, has no real or substantial relation to these objects, or is a palpable invasion of rights secured by the fundamental law, it is the duty of the courts so to adjudge, and thereby give effect to the Constitution.[63]

Operating from these premises, he said, the Court was able to sustain the Kansas statute because it was able to take judicial notice of the fact, "within the knowledge of all," that there was some sort of connection between the excessive use of intoxicating liquors on the one hand and crime and pauperism on the other.

Mugler v. *Kansas* seemed at the time to warrant two inferences: first, that the Court was at last ready to shoulder the burden of mediating between vested rights and the police power; secondly, that in doing so, it would require that state legislation seriously affecting vested rights be justified by facts known to all, and hence to courts. A year later in *Powell* v. *Pennsylvania*,[64] a closely similar case save for the fact that it involved oleomargarine instead of liquor, the Court repelled both these deductions, sustaining the challenged legislation on the ground that it could not say, on the basis of facts which it was entitled to notice judicially, that oleomargarine was not injurious to public health. It was no part of the judicial function, Justice Harlan added largely, to conduct investigations of fact touching "public policy merely" with a view either *"to sustaining or frustrating the legislative will"* thereon.[65]

So once again did judicial review under the Fourteenth Amendment encounter a check, but not a lasting one this time, as the statistics prove. During the first decade of the amendment only three cases were decided under all its clauses, and none was decided in the 1878 term; during the next decade, which brings us to *Powell* v. *Pennsylvania*, forty-six cases were so decided. Then, following 1896 the flood burst. Between that date and the end of the 1905 term of court, two hundred and ninety-seven cases were passed upon under the amendment—substantially all under the "due process" and "equal protection" clauses.[66] What was the cause of this inundation? In the main it is to be found in the Court's ratification of the idea, following a period of vacillation, that the term *lib-*

erty of the "due process" clause was intended to annex the principles of *laissez faire* capitalism to the Constitution and put them beyond reach of state legislative power.

IV.

PRIOR to the Civil War American constitutional law and theory evince a quite surprising unconcern regarding "liberty." Save for "liberty of speech and press," which usually had an article to itself in the various constitutional bills of rights, and liberty of the physical person, for which the usual *habeas corpus* clause was thought to provide a sufficient remedy, the term was left to the popular orators on the Fourth of July and to the Abolitionists.[67] So far as the power of the states was involved, in brief, liberty was the liberty which the *ordinary* law allowed and nothing more; nor did anyone ever think to suggest that a statute which curtailed the previous freedom of action of persons was for that reason "retrospective" or "retroactive."

The question of Freedmen's Rights, however, following the Civil War put the term on the way to acquire juristic significance, first by securing its insertion into the Fourteenth Amendment. The next step was Justice Bradley's dissent in the Slaughter House Cases, wherein, as we have seen, the term was held to connote a wide field of rights which heretofore had been subject to legislative definition; and then a few years later occurred the reiteration of this dissent as a "concurring opinion," in 111 *United States*. Contemporaneously, as it happened, the first enactments designed to protect employees against employers were finding their way to the state statute books and arousing the heated opposition of those who professed to believe that industrial *laissez faire* represented the order of Nature and of Nature's God.[68] To these and to the interests they spoke for, Justice Bradley's opinion, not to mention Conkling's argument in 116 *United States*, was as manna sent from heaven. But would the American judiciary regard it in the same favorable light? The debate spread through the state courts, through the federal circuits, to the law journals, then to the Supreme Court itself,[69] and gradually *laissez faire* won out, being assisted in the case of the Supreme Court by such opportune appointments as those of Justices Brewer and Peckham, the former of whom, especially, was ready at all times to inform the world how heartily he detested "the paternal theory of government,"[70] and assumed with the utmost naïveté that his pet aversion had in some providential fashion got into the Constitution without his helping to put it there.

So the word "liberty" of the Fourteenth Amendment became at last a judicially construable term in limitation of state legislative power; albeit at first in the restricted sense of "freedom of contract," by which was meant more specifically the freedom of employers to use their economic advantage to drive hard bargains with those seeking employment. "Liberty," in a word, became assimilated to property, that is to say, with *investment capital,* about which was thus cast an immunity far surpassing in scope any that had ever been dreamed of in the rustic philosophy of vested rights.[71]

And this purely proprietarian concept of "liberty" remained unmodified in our constitutional law until the war with Germany. Recent decisions spread the mantle of the amendment also over freedom of speech and the press, and, inferentially, other similar paraphernalia of political democracy. This development has been hailed as a "victory for liberalism on the Bench."[72] At least it brackets the term "property" in the "due process" clause with interests which are something other than an extension thereof. It also projects judicial review into new territory of unindicated extent.

And while the constitutional basis of judicial review was being thus expanded, private recourse to it was being very greatly facilitated by the increasing hospitality of the lower federal courts to injunction proceedings for suspending the enforcement of state laws alleged to violate the amendment. The objection to such a suit is that it is a suit against a state and hence barred by the Eleventh Amendment. The point was first raised in 1824 in the case of *Osborn* v. *Bank of the United States,*[73] and was met by Marshall by limiting the application of the amendment to suits "where a state is party to the record." Otherwise, said the Chief Justice, the national government would be powerless to protect its agents or enforce its laws in the face of intermeddling state officials except by proceedings brought after the mischief was done[74]—cogent reasoning enough from the point of view of national supremacy. The rule proved none the less to be too broad, and, in a suit brought a few years later against the governor of Georgia to recover money held by him in his official capacity, Marshall himself declined to follow it.[75] From this time on for many years the Court followed the doctrine that there is an essential difference between suits brought to *prevent* a state official from proceeding under a statute alleged to be unconstitutional and one brought to *compel* such an official to act *positively* in his official capacity; and while the Eleventh Amendment was held to forbid the federal courts from assuming jurisdiction in the latter on any pretext, the former were still considered to be within the judicial power of the United States.[76] And so matters stood when the Ayers Case reached the Court in 1887.[77] There, probably because of the confusing set of facts which confronted it, the Court held that a suit brought against state officers who had "no personal interest in the subject-matter of the suit," but solely to restrain them from proceeding under an alleged unconstitutional act, was a suit against the state. In short, the Osborn Case was virtually set aside—but not for long.

One of the most conspicuous features, so far as the law was concerned, of the advance of *laissez faire* in the late Eighties and early Nineties was the increasing favor with which the injunction was regarded by "the Interests." Nor is this strange. The historical use of the injunction is to protect *property*, and it is not ordinarily available against those from whom adequate damages would be collectible. Particularly did the famous Debs Case[78] in 1895 serve to advertise the potentialities of this judicial instrument as a substitute for the more democratic processes of government—an instrument capable of keeping labor in its place and not likely to be used to interfere with the "private initiative" of capital.

In a series of cases beginning at this same period involving the validity under the "due process" clause of the Fourteenth Amendment of railway rates set by state authority, the Court gradually elbowed the Ayers Case into the background and advanced *pari passu* its own claims to a supervisory rôle—which it had declined to assume in the Munn Case—over such rates.[79] Both developments were virtually completed by *Smyth* v. *Ames*,[80] decided in 1898. There the doctrine was announced that railway rates set by state authority must yield a "reasonable return"—that is, one adjudged by the Court to be *reasonable*—on the "fair value"—that is, one adjudged by the Court to be *fair*—of carrier's property devoted to intrastate commerce; and, furthermore, that a federal court was entitled, upon application by a carrier, to issue an injunction suspending the enforcement of rates set by state authority until their compliance with these specifications was finally attested

by the Supreme Court—a process which has frequently required many years.[81] And such, in the
main, is still the law and doctrine today affecting
state and local regulation of public utility rates.[82]

The logical difficulties which the Eleventh
Amendment opposes to such a result impudently
persist, nevertheless, even in the face of ultimate
authority. They are chiefly two. It is of course a
principle of Anglo-American law that an officer
who acts in excess of the law—which in this country includes the Constitution of the United States
—loses his official character. But in the present
situation this rule cuts both ways. For if the officer
is subject to judicial process on the ground that
his act was not that of a "state" in the sense of the
Eleventh Amendment, how can the same act be
deemed to be that of a "state" in the sense of the
Fourteenth Amendment; and yet if it is not the
latter, on what ground can redress be sought
against it, considering that the prohibitions of
the Fourteenth Amendment apply only to "state"
acts? One aspect of this conumdrum was once dealt
with by Chief Justice White. His opinion on the
subject leaves the law as it found it, but can hardly
be said to be dialectically satisfying.[83]

Much more instructive is the second difficulty.
Suppose—as has indeed happened more than once
—that a federal court enjoins enforcement of a
state act which the Supreme Court ultimately
holds to be constitutional—what has happened in
the interval? Obviously, the "judicial power of the
United States" has been "construed to extend to a

suit . . . in equity" against a state, and hence
contrary to the Eleventh Amendment. How can
such a result be vindicated? Inasmuch as it usually, if not always, takes place in connection with
suits brought under the "due process" clause of
the Fourteenth Amendment, one way of justifying
it would be to say that the later amendment had
modified the earlier one; but apparently the Court
does not favor that suggestion.[84] This being so,
there remains, so far as I can see, only one way of
explaining the seeming paradox just pointed out,
and that is by saying—with the proper qualifications regarding equity jurisdiction—that when a
state act is attacked as violative of the "due process" clause of the Fourteenth Amendment, *the former presumption in favor of the constitutionality
of state acts is automatically reversed.* Any state
official action under such a measure, if likely to be
to the serious detriment of property interests, becomes thereupon enjoinable by a federal court in
equity proceedings, and it takes a favorable decision of the Supreme Court to put the measure
back into force—if it ever was in force.[85] Nor, in
fact, is this the only indication which judicial review in support of the "due process" clause gives of
having cast off the restraint of a principle which
was once insisted upon as fundamental.[86]

We return, therefore, to the problem of factual
justification of state legislation under the Fourteenth Amendment. What business has the Court
with questions of this nature, what facilities has it
for handling them, how can it possibly presume to

pass upon a legislative determination of them; and yet, if it cannot, how is it to give any practical effect to the theory that the state's police power and the "due process" clause embody complementary concepts? In *Mugler* v. *Kansas*, as we have seen, the Court was able to sustain the act under review simply by taking notice of facts of common knowledge; but when in *Powell* v. *Pennsylvania* such justificatory facts were lacking, it reversed the process and sustained the challenged statute because no generally known facts showed it to be an infringement "of rights secured by fundamental law." This seesaw might have continued indefinitely, and the doctrine of judicial review stated in the Mugler Case have been kept a harmless piece of pageantry, but for the advance of *laissez faire*. The same impulse, however, which generated the concept of "freedom of contract" naturally carried with it an intention to make this concept effective. In *Holden* v. *Hardy*,[87] decided in 1898, the Court repeating its exploit in the Mugler Case, sustained an eight-hour law for miners on the basis of the knowledge it shared with the rest of mankind respecting the special drawbacks to health of this particular occupation. But when seven years later it was confronted in *Lochner* v. *New York*[88] with a ten-hour law for bakeries, it decided—by a majority of one—not to repeat its march down hill of the Powell Case. "To the common understanding," said Justice Peckham for the Court, "the trade of a baker has never been regarded as an unwholesome one"; and on this basis the New York statute was set aside as being not "a fair, reasonable, and appropriate exercise of the police power of the state," but a "meddlesome interference with the rights of the individual."[89]

Manifestly, the Lochner Case discards the principle of presumed constitutionality; nor was this for the moment only. In 1923 in the Minimum Wage Case,[90] a divided Court declared the following doctrine, which a few months subsequently a unanimous Court approved: "Freedom of contract is . . . the general rule and restraint the exception; and the exercise of legislative authority to abridge it can be justified only by the existence of exceptional circumstances."[91] In short, the burden of proof rests on the state. This, however, is only half the story. For during a part of the interval between the Lochner and the Adkins Cases, and especially between 1910 and 1920, the Court was generally dominated by a majority which was distinctly disinclined to interfere with state legislation on the basis of the Fourteenth Amendment, and whose members frequently asserted doctrine which to all practical intents and purposes was the doctrine of presumed constitutionality.[92] The result is that *the Court is able today to approach the question of factual justification from either one of two opposed angles, according as it wishes to sustain a statute or to overturn it, and is able to cite an ample array of precedents in justification of either approach.*

What is more, the Court has long since abandoned the cramped premises of the principle of "judicial notice" when dealing with questions of fact. The commencement of this interesting development was an argument of counsel in 1908 in the case of *Muller* v. *Oregon*,[93] which involved a ten-hour law for women in industrial employment. In defense of the act the future Justice Brandeis presented a brief which, after dismissing the relevant precedents in a meager three pages, devoted well over a hundred pages to statistics and other materials of scientific provenience showing the detrimental effects of protracted hours of physical labor upon women.[94] This impressive document persuaded even so convinced an individualist as Justice Brewer that the Court was entitled to notice the fact that "women are the mothers of the race" and not apt to be so rugged as men, and hence the statute was sustained.

In subsequent cases counsel have occasionally repeated the experiment of the so-called "Brandeis brief," sometimes successfully, more often not, since so elaborate a method of advocacy has not usually been employed except to combat the most stubborn prejudices of the controlling majority of the Bench.[95] On the other hand, that the Court has been pretty well rid of the aversion it earlier evinced to judicial investigations of facts is certain, and the credit may well go to the original inventor of the Brandeis brief, many of whose famous dissents follow the same model.[96] Both points are well illustrated in *Burns Baking Company* v. *Bryan*,[97] where in 1924 the Court set aside a Nebraska statute which required that bread be sold in pound and half-pound loaves, on its own independent finding that the allowance made by the statute for shrinkage of the loaves was too small. Entering upon an elaborate discussion of the entire process of bread-making, Justice Butler for the Court pronounced the act "unnecessary" for the protection of buyers against fraud and "essentially unreasonable and arbitrary." Justice Brandeis dissented, with an opinion still more elaborate. "It is not our province," he asserted, "to weigh evidence. Put at its highest, our function is to determine in the light of all facts which may enrich our knowledge and enlarge our understanding," whether the act of the legislature "transcends the bounds of reason."[98] It is apparent, therefore, that his disagreement with his brethren was not over the question of the Court's capacity to "conduct investigations of facts," but rather what constitute "the bounds of reason"—not infrequently a somewhat speculative question.

For the rest we can subscribe without qualification to Justice Brandeis' characterization of the decision in this case as "an exercise of the powers of a super-legislature."[99] Likewise, we can sympathize with Justice Holmes's declaration shortly before his retirement from the Bench three years ago, that he could discover "hardly any limit but the sky" to the Court's present power in disallowance of state acts "which may happen to strike a majority of this Court as for any reason undesirable."[100] He divulged, nevertheless, but half of the truth. For he could equally well have added that the Court has just as broad a discretion, so far at least as the Fourteenth Amendment is concerned, in *sustaining* legislation which may happen to strike a majority of its members as for any reason desirable. In a word, what "due process of law" today means in relation to state legislative power is *the approval of the Supreme Court.*

V.

"JUST as the twig is bent the tree's inclined." The process whereby state legislative power became at last subordinated to a discretionary supervision of the national Supreme Court was set going with the Constitution itself; but what has kept it going since then? The inertia of the many will answer for much; the management of the few will answer for more. Yet even when both these factors are taken into account, does not something still remain to be explained? Unless American democracy has been a myth, there must have been a degree of complicity on the part of the American people themselves.

There would seem to be no question that conditions of life have fostered among us a rather special regard for property and the property right. This regard has been widespread and has even been a force making for social understanding and democratic feeling. To the average man a modicum of prosperity has been a rational possibility, frequently realized. To the average man, moreover, property has always spelled security, "a warm corner in a cold universe"; while by a sort of pathetic fallacy he comes to regard in the same light the wealth of the rich and powerful, with whose peculiar anxieties he thus experiences a certain sympathy. More than that, great riches have represented with us some sort of personal achievement far oftener than otherwise; while the special favors of the law have gone unnoticed or have been treated as the legitimate spoils of those who knew their way about. Furthermore, while the vast resources of the country offered the most tremendous rewards, other stimulation to talent was conspicuously lacking. On the one hand, politics was disesteemed as the affair of everybody, the much ado about nothing to which in fact our political traditions and overcomplicated arrangements reduced it; on the other hand, art was almost nonexistent.

The question just raised therefore takes this form: how to account for the special concern of our constitutional law for the property interest when, on the whole, American democracy has been disposed to favor that interest? The answer is furnished by the outstanding feature of our constitutional system, the dispersion of legislative power among us. *The most persistent problem of American constitutional law arises from the fact that to a multiplicity of state legislatures has been assigned the most important powers of government over private rights.* And confronting this division of the normal competence of government has been a constantly increasing appreciation of the fact that *the basis of our prosperity is national.* It was this fact exactly which the Convention of 1787 deserves greatest credit for grasping. Jefferson endeavored to repudiate it, but in vain. His creed, inspiriting for its optimistic outlook upon average human nature, none the less resulted on the institutional side in disabling national power for social service, though not for serviceability to grafters and spoilers;[101] while at the same time it forwarded the interests of the most debased form of property, that in slaves. Then following the Civil War the even more intensely negative creed of capitalistic *laissez faire* laid its paralyzing hands on national policy. Yet at the same time the spread of capitalistic industry made more palpable than ever the fact that industrially, commercially, and economically we were one people, with one prosperity, one destiny. So, acting in response to this twofold stimulus, doctrinaire *laissez faire* and a truly realistic perception of the material sources of national greatness, the Supreme Court proceeded, under the "commerce" clause and the "due process" clause of the Fourteenth Amendment, to clear the field for a nation-wide industry and commerce, with the result of immunizing them both for the time being from all effective political control. Today, however, Nira warns us, this era is at an end. Nira asserts that *as rights have been nationalized, so must political power, upon which rights necessarily depend, be nationalized correspondingly.* The further question accordingly arises, in what manner and after what fashion our constitutional law is to accommodate itself to this irrefutable fact —a question which directs our attention to judicial review as it has operated in the national field in support of proprietarian interests.

Due in part to the comparative paucity of the national legislative product judicial review of national legislation has remained to this day episodic and sporadic, characterized by sudden interventions of the Court which were intended to save the country .from some terrible disaster or to confer upon it some miraculous good, but productive of few settled principles. In the Dred Scott Case the Court yielded by an unfortunate second thought to Justice Wayne's persuasion that it had in its grasp the opportunity to settle the constitutional issues arising out of the slavery question.[102] Of the same general pattern were the decisions in the Legal Tender Cases,[103] and the Income Tax Decision of 1895[104] was even more clearly so.

In this case the Court, correcting a "century of error," deliberately and of calculation withdrew the wealth of the country from effective national taxation. This avowed *volte face* from the trend of judicial doctrine for a hundred years was executed in response to Mr. Joseph Choate's clarion call to duty to the recreant tribunal. It was Mr. Choate's theory that the "direct tax" clauses were inserted "for the protection" of "accumulated property in the states as against the inroad of mere numbers" and comprised "the fundamental condition of the [then existing] states adopting the Constitution." Said he:

I have thought that one of the fundamental objects of all civilized government was the preservation of the rights

of private property. I have thought that it was the very
keystone of the arch upon which all civilized government
rests, and that this once abandoned, everything was at
stake and in danger. That is what Mr. Webster said in
1820 at Plymouth, and I supposed that all educated,
civilized men believed in that. According to the doctrines
that have been propounded here this morning, even that
great fundamental principle has been scattered to the
winds. . . . The act of Congress which we are impugn-
ing before you is communistic in its purposes and tendencies, and is defended here upon principles as communistic, socialistic—what shall I call them—populistic as
ever have been addressed to any political assembly in the
world.[105]

Confronted with the direct testimony in the
Hylton Case of a Justice who had personally par-
ticipated in the framing of the Constitution as to
the extremely limited purpose of the "direct tax"
clauses,[106] Mr. Choate's history savors of improvi-
sation. His psychology, however, was impeccable.
"Communistic march"—those were winged words,
and they found their way to the hearts of Chief
Justice Fuller and his four associates. "The present assault upon capital," proclaimed Justice
Field, "is but the beginning. It will be but the step-
ping-stone to others, larger and more sweeping,
till our political contests will become a war of the
poor against the rich; a war constantly growing in
intensity and bitterness."[107]

The veto of the Court held the sun and moon at
pause for seventeen years. Meantime, we hear no
more of the "direct tax" clauses. Having achieved
its immediate purpose with them, the Court retired

them into disuse once more, and that is where, except for the Stock Dividend Case,[108] they have continued to this day.[109]

But while cataclysmic assertions of judicial power have played no negligible part in the national field, it is rather to those slow accretions to judicial review which are accomplished by the operation of unnoted precedents, or what the Court may choose to treat as such, and still more, to those which are effected *by taking for granted propositions which have never been really argued*—it is to these that the informed critic will especially direct his attention. It was by taking for granted propositions never really argued that the Court brought itself at last to a position from which it felt warranted in denying that the Sixteenth Amendment gave Congress the power to tax previously exempted incomes.[110] It was by the same absent-minded procedure that the Court gradually strangulated Section 3224 of the Revised Statutes, declaring that "no suit for the purpose of restraining the assessment or collection of any tax should be maintained in any court," the lethal tug having been given only two years since.[111] So also it is by this method that the Court has apparently come to assume that the results which it has reached in application of the "due process" clause of the Fourteenth Amendment to local legislation are transferable without substantial modification to the like clause of the Fifth Amendment, as constitutional criteria of national legislative power.[112] This assumption is, to be sure, by no means baseless historically,[113] yet once it is examined it is found to encounter certain very serious objections.

1. When the Fifth Amendment was added to the Constitution in 1792, no one, so far as I am aware, had ever suggested that the term "due process of law" had any other than its anciently established and self-evident meaning of correct procedure; nor was such a suggestion to be accepted by any court, in any jurisdiction, for many years to come.[114]

2. And along with this historical objection goes a logical one. The police power is a general residual power of legislation which theoretically came into existence simply in consequence of the erection of the state legislature, and which, therefore, would be without any limitation whatsoever in relation to rights of person and property except for constitutional restraints prescribed for the purpose and judicial review to enforce these. The powers of Congress are on the other hand expressly conferred powers, many of which are confined to specified subject matter. Granting that there are anterior rights of the individual which constitute an exception to the otherwise pervasive "power to govern men and things," as Chief Justice Taney put it, the rule of construction which is thus invoked reciprocally exacts that the expressly granted powers of Congress be treated as a considered subtraction from indefinite prior rights of person and property. The more general yields to the more specific.

3. The fact of national unity yields a simi-

lar conclusion. Industrially and commercially the
country is, as I have reiterated, a single community; politically it is a single public—thanks to
radio, telegraph, telephone, a single *publicity.*
That the range of governing authority which is
connoted by the term "police powers" should be
parceled out in such a community among forty-
eight autonomous centers is an anomaly which
must long since have become utterly impracticable
but for the enforcement by the Supreme Court of
certain uniform standards of legislative conduct
in relation to property, business, and commerce.
Thus the very reason which above all others suggested judicial review of state legislation at the
outset, goes far to validate its indefinite extension
within recent years under the Fourteenth Amendment. For a general judicial supervision of the national legislative power manifestly no such argument is forthcoming. An act of Congress is itself a
rule of uniformity, or it is an announcement by
Congress of its judgment of how far circumstances
make uniformity desirable. To urge the claims of
judicial review in such a case is not to vindicate
the cause of uniformity but the contrary. It is to
pit one conception of uniformity, the Court's,
against another conception, that of Congress.

4. This consideration, obvious in itself, is
thrown into higher relief by Nira; and it is also in
the light shed from the same source that some of
the more specific concepts which the Court has developed in testing state power under the Fourteenth Amendment become clearly unworkable or

irrelevant when set up as tests of national power. A glaring illustration of this is afforded by the doctrine of "affectation with a public interest." What is a business affected with a public interest if it is not a business which affects a public interest? And is not interstate commerce a public interest? So much so is it that Congress alone may regulate it. But as we have seen, Nira conceives of the interstate commercial activity as one phase, albeit a dominating one, of an industrial *continuum*, with the result that its welfare is intertwined with, and dependent upon, that of business activity as a whole. Yet, unless it is prepared to challenge this premise, the Court can scarcely assert that a particular business, linked up with the entire industrial set-up, is not one affected with a public interest. The question is clearly one of degree, and while the Court is constantly called upon by modern doctrines of constitutional law to determine such questions,[115] yet it ought to be sure that it has at hand the facts which will enable it to do so understandingly. Furthermore, the Court has shown itself slow to require exceptions to be made which would jeopardize a legislative scheme of which it approves as a whole.[116]

5. And finally, even more irrelevant, if possible, to the solution of the questions of governmental power raised by the New Deal are the ideas of property which underlie the doctrine of vested rights and the derived doctrine of due process of law. Stripped of their more outrageously theological and animistic trappings, these ideas boil down

to two: first, that property is the reward of well-directed personal effort, and a necessary reward if the services of a civilized society are to be maintained; secondly, that it is the basis of private security, and hence of a stable polity.[117] That these ideas once represented valid hypotheses of constitutional interpretation need not be disputed—the point is that modern conditions subordinate them to an entirely different set of ideas. In the words of Professor Dewey, "from the stand-point of modern economic theory, the most surprising thing about modern industry is the small number of persons who have any effective interest in the acquisition of wealth."[118] On the other hand, with what has happened in this country since 1929 still fresh in mind, few can have the hardihood to question that the outstanding characteristic of wealth today is that it is a function of social process, so that when social process falters, wealth simply vanishes into thin air, leaving an impoverished society.[119] Nor is the vast proportion of the wealth owned in the American community today primarily a source of private security—it is a source of *power* over other people's lives, and of a kind of power which has never hesitated to thwart or corrupt the processes of political democracy in order to secure its own purposes.[120]

But if this is a just account of matters, how can it possibly be contended that the doctrines which the Court has set up as a test of local legislation have any but a very limited pertinence to a scheme of legislation having the purpose and scope of

Nira and her sisters? This legislation—and even more the conditions which gave birth to it—throw questions of governmental power into an entirely new perspective to which the whole pattern of constitutional law must be adjusted sooner or later, and sooner rather than later.

Happily, recent decisions of the Court evince unmistakable recognition of this necessity. The opinion of Justice Roberts in the New York Milk Case is,[121] indeed, no less than revolutionary when put alongside the type of constitutional law which the Court has been handing down the past decade and a half. It reasserts the necessary predominance of the public interest over all private rights of property and contract if government is to remain a going concern. It leaves the once portentous concept of "business affected with a public interest" sadly deflated, rejecting the idea that there is something "peculiarly sacrosanct about the price one may charge for what he sells or makes," and it proclaims that so far as the "due process" clause is concerned, "a state is free to adopt whatever economic policy may reasonably be deemed to promote public welfare."[122] While, in view of the special prerogative that courts are apt to assert over the meaning of words, this language may not be altogether free from ambiguity, still its general tendency seems reasonably clear. This, as I should put it, is to meet the problem which I have just been discussing not by differentiating between the two "due process" clauses, but rather by paring down judicial review of state legislation under the

Fourteenth Amendment to such an extent that the parallel application of the Fifth Amendment would not materially embarrass the national legislature's freedom of judgment and action. Perhaps for the time being this is the better solution—certainly it is a democratic one.

To sum up briefly: The special position of the property right in our constitutional system was premised on a theory and on an antagonistic fact. The theory was that the true basis of American prosperity was national. The fact was that legislative power in the United States was parceled out among a multiplicity of legislatures. The dilemma thus resulting was met by the American judiciary during the first forty years of our national existence by the establishment of judicial review as a means of controlling legislative power and its extension by the doctrine of vested rights. Meantime the economic maturing of the country was proceeding at very unequal rates of speed in the different sections, partly on account of the rapid advance of the frontier, partly on account of slavery. To meet this condition of diversity the ebullient Jacksonian Democracy brought forth the concept of the police power, and for the first time quiescent notions of government were challenged in the name of popular sovereignty, though chiefly in the local forum. The Civil War and its aftermath imposed new conditions on the nation's development, although just how these were to be translated into constitutional law long remained uncertain. The rapid advance of capitalistic individualism, the multiplied pressures which this was capable of bringing to bear, and finally the immense prestige which the *laissez faire* political economy and cosmology came at one period to enjoy, finally turned the scales so far as the Supreme Court was concerned. Beginning with the later Eighties the Court set about elaborating the "due process" clause of the Fourteenth Amendment into a doctrinal network capable of enmeshing state power in every direction, an achievement which the American democracy tolerated, even welcomed, in the name of prosperity. But in this very process, and as part and parcel of it, the Court also developed a technique in the handling of constitutional problems which in the vast majority of critical situations leaves it free to do about as it chooses. Judicial review in the sense of judicial discretion has devoured its progeny, constitutional law; and by the same sign, "due process of law" is no Frankenstein's monster that rides down legislation in defiance of its creator's will—it is the servant of the Court's *legislative* judgment. Were Nira and her kin to perish at the Court's hands, it would not be by the decree of "some brooding omnipresence in the sky,"[123] but of a majority of nine entirely human beings.

CHAPTER III

"A GOVERNMENT OF LAWS AND NOT OF MEN" IN A COMPLEX WORLD

I.

THE "founding fathers" owed their mental sustenance much more largely to seventeenth-century England than to the England with which they were themselves contemporary. Locke's influence upon them was, of course, immense; and the venerable stereotype which furnishes the title of this chapter similarly testifies to their favorite reading. The phrase "a government of laws and not of men," or "an empire of laws and not of men," occurs repeatedly in Harrington's *Oceana*,[1] whence it found its way into the Massachusetts constitution of 1780 and nearly a quarter century later into Chief Justice Marshall's opinion in *Marbury* v. *Madison*. Harrington himself had but skimmed the cream from a passage in Aristotle's *Politics*.[2]

What has been the influence of this maxim upon American constitutional law and theory? The question will be discussed in relation to "legislative power," "judicial power," and "executive power"; and again we shall find it pertinent to turn to the New Deal for the elucidation of some recent trends.

In urging his fellow citizens to *Have Faith in*

Massachusetts in 1919, the late Calvin Coolidge
wrote: "Men do not make laws. They do but discover them. . . . That State is most fortunate in
its form of government which has the aptest instruments for the discovery of law."[3]

From this point of view, obviously, legislative
power, in the sense of the *right* of certain human
beings to impose their *will* upon their fellows,
simply does not exist. Legislation there is, to be
sure, but it is not an act of *will* or *power*, but one
of *discovery* and *declaration* of principles which
are entitled to prevail because of their own intrinsic excellence. More than two thousand years before Coolidge, Demosthenes had voiced the same
thought: "Every law is a discovery, a gift of God,
a precept of wise men,"[4] a thought which recurs in
Aristotle's *Ethics* and, centuries later, in Cicero's
De Republica.[5] In the Middle Ages, till a late date,
no alternative idea presents itself.[6] Even the re-
doubtable Hobbes dares not flout this idea of law
outright. In the same chapter of the *Leviathan* to
which the so-called "Positive School of Jurisprudence" is wont to trace its own rise, the celebrated
definition of "civil law" as "a command" is immediately followed by the statement that "the law of
nature and the civil law contain each other and are
of equal extent."[7] And a similar pietism is adopted
by Blackstone a century later: Parliament is "omnipotent"; but its acts are merely declaratory of
natural law[8]—a piece of obscurantism to which
Bentham paid his respects with devastating effect
in the *Fragment on Government.*[9] Meantime, Otis

in his *Rights of the British Colonies Asserted and Proved* had assailed the Blackstonian conception from the opposite angle: even omnipotency could not make 2 and 2, 5. "The supreme power in a state is *jus dicere* only—*jus dare*, strictly speaking, belongs alone to God."[10]

In our own day we are witnessing the efforts of the physical sciences to cast off what some of their disciples have come to regard as the thraldom of a belief in a natural law of phenomena.[11] At the same time there are lawyers and publicists who would gladly reassert their claim to the term, by no means forgetting the reinforced prestige which its scientific employment has given it.[12] Thus the notion that the anonymous forces of the market constitute a species of "higher law" having at once the characteristics of a *moral* law which is binding on the consciences of statesmen and of a *scientific* law which is capable of vindicating itself against any who may ignore or defy it, is of the very essence of *laissez faire*, and clearly underlies—to take a current illustration—the Honorable John W. Davis' recent attack on the New Deal.[13] Mr. Davis puts this question: "Who can doubt that there are natural laws in the social and economic as well as the physical worlds, and that these cannot be overridden without courting disaster?" Mr. Davis overlooks the fact that the physical sciences see their laws "overridden" constantly, not only without disaster but with enormous benefit to mankind. The steam engine "overrides" the law of the expansion of gases, the parachute "overrides" the law of fall-

ing bodies—to say nothing of that humble article
of attire, a pair of suspenders! Nor indeed is it
easy to believe that Mr. Davis has passed his life
giving legal advice to the "natural laws" of "the
economic world" rather than to human beings who
were endeavoring—and often quite successfully—
to take advantage of such "laws" for their own
benefit. Yet if individuals can do this, there would
seem to be *a priori* no reason why the public cannot do the same thing through the agency of government.[14]

The classic texts of the idea of law as *an expression of human will and power* hail from the Roman
law.[15] The maxim *"salus populi suprema lex"* is
one of these; another is the phrase *"vox populi,
vox dei"*; still another is the famous passage from
Institutes: "What hath pleased the prince has the
force of law, inasmuch as . . . the people conferred upon him all their power and rulership."[16]

The notion, therefore, that there is some quality
in the people at large which enables them to im-
part the obligatory force of law to their desires
when those are expressed in a certain way, harks
back to the Roman *Comitia;* and was a deduction,
one conjectures, from that long-drawn-out series
of statutes (*leges*), or treaties, whereby patricians
and plebeians were finally welded into a single society. And so, too, was the emergence of the notion
of legislative sovereignty in England the consequence of social commotion and reconstruction, of
the breakup of "the cake of custom." Writing at
the close of the English Reformation, Sir Thomas

Smith described Parliament's power as "absolute":

The Parliament abrogateth old laws, maketh new, giveth orders for things past and for things hereafter to be followed. . . . That which is done by this consent is called firm, stable and sanctum, and is taken for law. . . . All that ever the people of Rome might do either in the *comitiis centuriatis* or *tributis,* the same may be done by the Parliament of England which representeth and hath the power of the whole realm, both the head and the body. For every Englishman is intended to be there present, either in person or by procuration and attorneys.[17]

Thanks to the current influence of Blackstone, the notion of legislative sovereignty also made a formidable bid for acceptance in the first American constitutions, and this despite the fact that many of these instruments gave the most explicit recognition in accompanying bills or declarations of rights to the theory of a transcendental law of justice, protective of the fundamental rights of the individual. The compromise which was worked out between these logically contradictory ideas in the course of the first half century of our constitutional history marks, nevertheless, an almost unqualified victory for the secular conception of law. The ordinary legislature is not, it is true, the constitutional equivalent of the people; it is only a subordinate political agency, whose enactments must accord with the constitution as interpreted judicially. But the legal supremacy of the constitution is due to its being the ordinance of the sovereign *will* of the people rather than to its *content*.[18]

Despite which, when we turn to consider the significance of *"judicial power"* in a "government of laws and not of men," we again find ourselves in the atmosphere of the conception of law as something not made but declared, though forced at the same moment to take account of an important distinction. The notion that law exists independently of human will and only awaits discovery presents itself, one perceives, in two forms. Demosthenes, speaking with Draco, Solon, and Lycurgus in mind, described the act of discovery as that of "wise men." Cicero, on the other hand, writing from the point of view of the Stoic notion of the equality of man, regarded *"lex naturalis"* as addressed to the reason of mankind at large, and from this premise drew the conclusion that *lex naturalis* was *self-interpreting*.[19] A comparable idea recurs in the history of religious faith again and again. Constantine the Great at the Council of Nicea enthroned the Bible as "the Infallible Judge of Truth"; and, as Professor Allen points out in his *Political Thought of the Sixteenth Century,* the prolific source of Protestant sectarianism was the notion that "the Scriptures speak unmistakably."[20] That the counterpart of this naïve theory should appear in due course in the field of constitutional interpretation was a matter of course. The Civil War was fought over two unmistakable readings of the Constitution; and only the other day we find Justice Sutherland, in his dissent to the Minnesota Moratorium Case, invoking the same idea repeatedly.[21] Nor do certain of Nira's critics, e.g., the Liberty League, rely on anything better. Why not be honest, they say, and admit that Nira can be legitimated only by constitutional amendment? A very edifying attitude, no doubt, but would those who assume it support such an amendment? In Gibbon's once famous phrase, "a melancholy doubt obtrudes itself upon the reluctant mind."[22]

But while the notion of the self-interpreting document, which would render one man's interpretation of the Constitution equally valid with that of any other,[23] undoubtedly aided the initial establishment of judicial review, it does not furnish the official justification of that institution—on the contrary, it logically contradicts the latter. Again we may turn with profit to English constitutional history.

The knowledge which men in general have of the laws of England, wrote Fortescue in his *De Laudibus Legum Angliae*, of customs, statutes, acts of Parliament, maxims, and the law of nature, can be but superficial, comparable with that which they have of "faith, love, charity, the sacraments, and God's commandments," while leaving "other mysteries in Divinity to those who preside in the Church." Hence it is that the Prince should always pronounce judgment through his courts, inasmuch as "for that expertness in the laws the which is requisite for judges, the studies of twenty years barely suffice." And the lesson with which Fortescue sought to instil his Prince, Coke found occasion a century and a quarter later to read his sovereign in more authoritative tones. Arguing that the judges were but his delegates, and furthermore that the "law was founded on reason, and that he and others had reason, as well as the judges," James I demanded to know why he should not decide cases in person if he took it into his mind to do so. Speaking for the judges, Coke soon exposed the fallacy of this childish philosophy: "Causes which concern the life—or goods—of his subjects are not be decided by natural reason, but by the artificial reason and judgment of the law, which law is an art which requires long study and experience before that a man can attain to the cognizance of it." In short, from being the universal inheritance of mankind, its distinctive inheritance, because attesting man's participation in the divine reason, law had become a *professional,* nay, an *official mystery.*[24]

Coke had hoped, perhaps, to restore to England the constitution of the early Lancastrians, centering about the name and fame of Magna Charta, whereof the courts, and especially the High Court of Parliament, were the chosen guardians.[25] Though the effort failed, it became one of the wellsprings of our own constitutional theory. The fount, however, is not the stream; from another source emerges a current which has imparted an entirely different coloration to the tradition which sets toward us from Coke and Locke. I mean Montesquieu's doctrine of the separation of powers. As

I pointed out in the previous chapter, American application of this principle early came to be controlled by the practical objective of curtailing state legislative power. The pivotal proposition was set up that between the *making* of law and its *construction* was an intrinsic difference of the most vital nature; and that since the latter function was demonstrably a daily concern of courts, it followed necessarily that the legislature might not perform it in a way to produce finally binding results.

Applied to the Constitution, this reasoning automatically produces judicial review. As Marshall insists in *Marbury* v. *Madison*, the Constitution, a solemn act of the people themselves, was made to be *preserved*, and no organ of government may alter its terms. But interpretation, which belongs to the courts exclusively and is "their peculiar and proper province,"[26] does not *change* the law, it *conserves* it. By the same token, judicial interpretation of the Constitution is vested with the authority of the Constitution itself.

"A government of laws and not of men" means, therefore, when viewed from the angle of the doctrine of the separation of powers, the theoretical *expulsion* from our inherited legal tradition of the notion that "legislative power" comprehends a power of law-declaring[27]—the very power with which it was originally identified! To effect this expulsion was, indeed, the first fruits of judicial review, and the continuance of judicial review has been dependent upon this outcome. The two things have supported each other; and without such reciprocal support neither could have long endured.

For all that, the notion of a judicial monopoly of the power to interpret the Constitution with finality has been repeatedly challenged and often with actual success. The doctrine of political questions signalizes an early concession by the Court itself at the expense of the strict logic of judicial review,[28] while it has repeatedly abandoned earlier doctrines óf its own in deference to so-called "practical constructions" of the Constitution as represented in the practice of the other departments.[29] On the theoretical side both Jefferson and Jackson turned the principle of the separation of powers against the doctrine of the finality of the Court's version of the Constitution by stressing the constitutional equality and mutual independence of the three departments; and while Webster denounced this course of reasoning as more calamitous than even the Calhounist doctrine of nullification, as more conducive to anarchy, yet Lincoln in his criticism of the Dred Scott Case followed Jackson, not the latter's Whig critic.[30]

Furthermore, when we turn to the statute book, we find that Congress has repeatedly undertaken to *declare* law with the definite intention of binding the courts. The act of 1855 declaring persons born abroad to be citizens of the United States was such a statute;[31] as also was the act of 1868 asserting the right of expatriation.[32] Both these acts altered the common law as it had been determined by the courts. Section 6 of the Clayton Act declaring labor not to be a "commodity" is still another illustration,[33] and so is the pronouncement of the recent Norris–La Guardia Act against "yellow-dog" contracts.[34] And several of the salient provisions of Nira reduce to the same type. They constitute a legislative definition of fair methods of competition and little more.[35]

Nor when the constitutional views of Congress and those of the Court have clashed is it the latter which have usually prevailed in the long run. It took a war to override the Dred Scott decision in its entirety. *Hepburn* v. *Griswold* was promptly overturned by the Court itself—possibly after it had been remade for the purpose. The Income Tax Decision was repealed by a constitutional amendment, although just how completely seems still to be a question. The present standing of the decisions in the first Child Labor Case and in the District of Columbia Minimum Wage Case is at least precarious. Clearly Congress has proved a better prophet than the Court of what the law has become, and so by the pragmatic test the better law-declaring body.

In short, it has not been practicable even in the case of Congress to divorce the law-declaring from the law-making function. Has it, on the other hand, been possible to divorce the law-making from the law-declaring function in the case of the judiciary?

II.

A passage in Cicero's *De Legibus*, the substance of which was later recalled by Coke, describes the law as "the silent magistrate" and the magistrate as "the law speaking."[36] Despite the apparent implication of these words, the Roman law would seem to have regarded interpretation as primarily an extension and continuation of the process of law-making, as the maxim *"cuius est condere est interpretari"*[37] appears to bear witness. Reciprocally, the official attitude of the common law has not always escaped skeptical comment. A Year-Book of the fourteenth century records a dispute among the judges over whether they were enforcing *reason* or only their own *will*,[38] and two hundred years later we find an Elizabethan bishop asserting flatly: "Whoever hath an absolute authority to interpret any written or spoken laws, it is he who is truly the law-giver to all intents and purposes, and not the person who first wrote or spoke them."[39] Suppose the good bishop had known of the Constitution of the United States, a law first spoken in 1789 and subject 150 years later to the "absolute authority" of the Supreme Court to interpret it!

Nowadays those who sustain the thesis that the judges do make law, notwithstanding the burden of proof presumably resting on them, universally put on the complacent smile of self-conscious victory. The case, nevertheless, as it is usually argued, is by no means so conclusive as it is often supposed to be. Given the inherent capacity of words to take on new meanings, the ordinary rules of logical discourse and the rules of documentary (i.e., statutory) construction, and given further the reasonable assumption that the lawmaker wrought with all these in mind—reënacting them, as it were, as part and parcel of the law itself— and it may become rather difficult to refute the Blackstonian dogma that interpretation preserves a preëxisting rule of law and does not make a new one.

The fact before which the doctrine of judicial automatism crumbles is not the fact that judges have viscera and emotions.[40] Nor is it the fact that courts have frequently given approval to shockingly bad pieces of logic, indicative as this may be of predetermination. The judicial function is essentially a syllogistic one, and "freedom of judicial decision" is something vastly more important than freedom to argue badly from accepted premises.[41] It is, rather, freedom to choose, within limits, the premises themselves; and hence asserts itself not *after* but *before* the juristic grounds of a decision are determined upon; and the rules of formal logic are its usual ally, not its usual enemy.

What gives the *coup de grâce* to the idea that— in the words of Chief Justice Marshall—"courts are the mere instruments of the law and can will nothing,"[42] is the simple fact that most so-called "doubtful cases" could very evidently have been decided just the opposite way to which they were decided without the least infraction of the rules of logical discourse or the least attenuation of the principle of *stare decisis*.

In other words, the judicial solution of doubtful cases is not to be explained solely by reference to the juristic materials on which such solution purports to rest. These materials from the outset furnish *legally* adequate basis for a pro-plaintiff solution and similarly adequate materials for a pro-defendₐnt solution. In this situation the court was not only presented with the opportunity, it was presented with the *necessity*, of making a choice between two bodies of juristic materials of approximately equal respectability and weight, and it did so, with the inevitable result of expressing a preference and of forwarding views as to which the law had hitherto preserved neutrality.

In short, *decision is choice; the very circumstance which produces doubtful cases guarantees the Court what Justice Holmes has termed "the sovereign prerogative of choice" in deciding them.* This circumstance may be described as a factual situation which forthwith divides, as it were, the acknowledged body of established law so far as it bears upon the said facts into two opposed—two antinomous—camps.

But if antinomy is the basis of judicial decision generally, emphatically is it the basis of judicial review and so of constitutional law. The game of dichotomization, if I may so term it, began, indeed, in the Convention which framed the Constitution. A complexus of compromises between opposed interests, the Constitution proffered from the outset a favorable soil for the utmost diversity of speculation regarding its nature and purpose. This, however, is only the commencement of the story, for the vast proportion of constitutional law maintains a tenuous connection, indeed, with the phraseology of the printed document.

The Constitution contains about thirty-five hundred words, "reading time" about twenty minutes. But hardly 2 per cent of this phraseology is of major significance to the student of constitutional law. A large proportion of the thousands of cases in which constitutional law is embodied stem upward from the foundational document in three or four slight phrases—the "due process" clauses, the "commerce" clause, the "obligation of contracts" clause. And what is the activating cause of this vast proliferation of cases? It is the speculations just mentioned concerning the nature and purpose of the Constitution and the interests which directly or indirectly prompt such speculations.

And this, of course, spells antinomy, dichotomy, for theories regarding the nature and purpose of the Constitution are rare, indeed, which were not formulated in answer to some other theory already formulated or at least perceived to be logically tenable. However, before dichotomy in constitutional theory can enter the sacred precincts of constitutional law something further must happen. Antagonistic theories must have undergone the sacramental and transforming laying on of hands of the Court—must, that is, be reflected in cases which, not having been overruled, furnish an eligible basis for argument by counsel.

By way of illustration let us turn for a moment

to certain familiar principles of constitutional
construction. We see at once that they fall into
pairs of opposites. Should the Constitution be construed "strictly" or "liberally"? That depends
logically on whether it came from the people at
large or from state sovereignties. Then there is the
antinomy of "inclusive" versus "exclusive" construction—in *Marbury* v. *Madison* Chief Justice
Marshall invoked the latter principle, in *McCulloch* v. *Maryland* he invoked the former. Again
there is the issue whether the Court's mandate to
interpret the Constitution embraces the power and
duty of adapting it to changed circumstances.
Marshall thought that it did, while Taney repudiated any such mission for the Court; and in the
recent Minnesota Moratorium Case the Chief Justice takes as his point of departure Marshall's doctrine, while Justice Sutherland, dissenting, builds
upon Taney's doctrine. Furthermore, there are
those diverse attitudes of a shifting majority of
the Bench which, though they may never have
found clear-cut expression in antithetical principles of constitutional construction, have given
rise none the less to conflicting courses of decision,
the potential bases of future opposed arguments
which either counsel or the Court may adopt without incurring professional reproach.[43] *In brief,
alternative principles of construction and alternative lines of precedent constantly vest the Court
with a freedom virtually legislative in scope in
choosing the values which it shall promote through
its reading of the Constitution.*

Two objections occur, however, and must be met, to the above account of things. The first arises from the very rational possibility that a judge may conscientiously endeavor to govern his choices by a sense of loyalty to the past. This, for instance, is undoubtedly what Chief Justice Taney had in mind to convey when he asserted in his opinion in the Dred Scott Case that the Constitution "speaks not only in the same words, but with the same intent" as when it came from its framers, and that "any other rule of construction would abrogate the judicial character" of the Court, "and make it the mere reflex of the popular opinion and passion of the day."[44] But this very illustration is sufficient to prove that judicial professions of such an attitude should usually be accepted *cum grano salis*, to say the least. Even at the time Justice Curtis offered a most devastating critique of the Chief Justice's history, while subsequent criticism has left the latter's ambitious essay hardly a leg to stand on. Indeed, at one point, and that a vital one, he departs from the course of historical fact so flagrantly that one can hardly believe that he did not do so knowingly. This is where he boldly invokes the "due process" clause of Amendment V as invalidating section 8 of the Missouri Compromise. As was pointed out in the previous chapter, no one at the time of the framing and adoption of the Constitution had any idea that this clause did more than consecrate a method of procedure against accused persons, and the modern doctrine of due process of law, the most important single basis of judicial review today, could never have been laid down except in defiance of history.[45] Nor did Taney himself scruple on occasion to subordinate the historical test to other considerations, as is evidenced by his opinion in the case of the *Genessee Chief*,[46] in which on grounds of convenience, slightly veneered with an appeal to history, the Court, rejecting the pertinent doctrine of common law and overturning a decision by Chief Justice Marshall, held that the federal admiralty jurisdiction was not confined to waters subject to the ebb and flow of the tide. Indeed, judicial researches into history for the purpose of establishing the intention of a vanished law-giver are almost always highly speculative enterprises, and necessarily so. Had the law-giver in question conceived of the situation before the Court and formed an intention respecting it, he would doubtless have expressed such intention unmistakably; and where the law-giver wrought a century and a half ago, such a quest becomes purely illusory. Compared with it, the ancient wheeze, "If you *had* a brother, would he like cheese," achieves an unexpected sobriety.[47]

Secondly, it may be objected that the above argument overlooks entirely the force of the doctrine of *stare decisis;* and it must be admitted that a rigid adherence to this doctrine might well have the result eventually of curtailing materially the freedom which the Court derives from the presence of alternative principles of construction and alternative theories of the nature and purposes of the

Constitution. But in the first place, the force of
the doctrine is constantly avoided by the alternative doctrine, which has been repeatedly illustrated
in recent years, that the Court is free to review
its own previous decisions for error. Indeed, in
proportion as judicial review has grown and expanded, the principle of *stare decisis* has progres-
sively lost operative force in the field of constitutional law,[48] and for good reason, inasmuch as the
most striking phases of this development took
place just as the country was definitely emerging
from the relatively simple conditions of an agricultural community into the relatively complex conditions of modern industrialism. Such being the
case, the substitution of "judicial discretion" as it
is conceived by the common law—in other words,
a discretion confined by the principle of *stare decisis*—for legislative discretion, was simply out of
the question, as the recent decision in *Nebbia* v.
New York goes far to prove. On this occasion, Mr.
Beck laments, the Court "calmly discarded its decisions of fifty years, and did not even pay these
decisions the obsequious respect of a funeral ora-
tion."[49] This is something of an exaggeration, no
doubt; "fifteen years" would have been much
nearer the truth than "fifty." The outstanding
fact, nevertheless, remains, that the decision makes
it more difficult than ever to regard the doctrine of
stare decisis as a factor of first importance in constitutional law.

Nor need the Court always override previous

decisions—whether by "silent suppression" or otherwise—in order to avoid being cramped by them. Aside from the circumstance that embarrassing holdings may be occasionally explained away plausibly as having been "*obiter*," the Court always has at hand the immensely important power to manipulate the differentiating facts of each fresh situation with a view to "distinguishing" it from previous cases. Thus, in effect, is the freedom which is lost through one decision as constantly regained in the next.[50]

Yet I would not be misunderstood; I am by no means asserting that the Court's reading of the Constitution has not possessed over extended periods a large degree of continuity and inner coherency. But this on examination will be usually found to result from the persistence of large general ideas of policy and of the interests thus protected rather than from the principle of *stare decisis*. For the rest, if precedent is a hurdle to the judicial lawmaker, so also is it a screen. Once choice has been made between two alternative lines of decision the new decision is immediately assimilated to the line selected and so every appearance of choice on the part of the Court automatically occulted even to the Court itself.

Likewise, once choice has been made between two competing principles of constitutional construction or of "higher law," one of them has been vindicated, and the Court is entitled to say that it has enforced a preëxisting rule of law, which is the

very definition of judicial function. On the other
hand, it is not entitled to say that this is *all* that it
has done. It has also exercised what by equally authoritative definition is *legislative power*. It has,
unavoidably, chosen between two lines of policy
and thereby expressed its preference for the line
chosen.[51]

The concept of "a government of laws" simmers
down, therefore, under the Constitution to a power
in the Supreme Court which is without statable
limits to set the metes and bounds of political authority in both the nation and the states. But the
dominating characteristic of judicial review, wide-
ranging though it be, is that it is ordinarily a
negative power only—a power of *refusal*. The
Court can forbid somebody else to act but cannot,
usually, act itself; in the words of Professor
Powell, it "can unmake the laws of Congress, but
cannot fill the gap." Present-day outlook, however,
as expressed in Nira and her kindred measures, requires that government assert an *active* rôle in the
supervision of matters which have been heretofore
left exclusively, or nearly so, to private initiative
and the forces of the market; while at the same
time the fluidity and complexity of such matters
under modern conditions generally exclude the
possibility of forecasting governmental action in
rules of law which go much into detail. We are
thus brought to consider the second term of the
antinomy, "a government of laws" *versus* "a government of men"—in other words, *"executive
power."*

III.

THE earliest repositories of executive power in this country were the provincial governors. Being the point of tangency and hence of irritation between imperial policy and colonial particularism, these officers aroused a widespread unpopularity that was easily generalized into distrust of their office, and this distrust was further aggravated by American explanation of the Revolution, that it was the outgrowth of the corruption of Parliament by the British King. So when Jefferson asserted in his *Summary View*, in 1774, that the King "is no more than the chief executive of the people, appointed by the laws and circumscribed with definite powers, to assist in working the great machine of government," he voiced a theory of executive power which, impudently as it flouted historical fact, had the support of those who drew the first American constitutions. In these instruments the governors were for the most part elected annually by the legislative assemblies, were stripped of every prerogative of their predecessors in relation to legislation, and were forced to exercise the powers left them subject to the advice of a council chosen also by the assembly, and from its own members if it so desired. Finally, out of abundant caution the constitution of Virginia stipulated that executive powers were to be exercised "according to the laws of" the Commonwealth, and that no power or prerogative was ever to be claimed "by virtue of any law, statute or custom of England."[52] "Executive power" was, in other words, left entirely to legislative definition and was cut off from all resources of the common law and the annals of English royalty.

But, fortunately or unfortunately, the older tradition of executive power was not to be exorcised so easily. Historically this tradition traces to the fact that the royal prerogative was residual power, that the monarch was first on the ground, that the other powers of government were offshoots from monarchical power, while their repositories were originally simply the delegates of the King or were his advisors, as in the time-worn formula they still are. Moreover, when our forefathers turned to Roman history, as they constantly did, it was borne in upon them that dictatorship had once been considered a normal feature of republican institutions.[53]

And what history consecrated, doctrine informed with vitality in 1776. The theorist of the American Revolution *par excellence* was John Locke, and Locke's notion of the royal prerogative was far from that of American Whiggism. "Though," wrote Locke in his *Treatise on Civil Government*, "Though—the executive and federative power of every community [the power, that is, "of war and peace, leagues and alliances, and all the transactions with all persons and communities without the commonwealth"] be really distinct in themselves, yet they are hardly to be separated and placed at the same time in the hands of distinct persons," inasmuch as both of them require "the force of society for their exercise."[54]

As presented to the outside world, that is, executive power *is* the state; what is it in its domestic aspect? Locke's answer to this important question is very arresting, and, indeed, at first perplexing. As the most casual reader of his pages must have gathered, the basic principle of the Lockian constitutional system is the supremacy of the legislative power. But just because of this principle, which guarantees the ultimate responsibility of the executive, Locke is enabled to attribute to the latter the broadest scope in relation to the standing law. Thus he defines "prerogative" as the power "to act according to discretion, for the public good, without the prescription of the law and sometimes against it." This power belongs to the executive, it being "impossible to foresee and so by laws to provide for all accidents and necessities that may concern the public, or make such laws as will do no harm if they are executed with inflexible rigor." Nor is this "undoubted prerogative" ever questioned, "for the people are very seldom or never scrupulous or nice in the point" whilst the prerogative "is in any tolerable degree employed for the use it was meant—that is, the good of the people."[55]

Thus, when the Convention of 1787 foregathered at Philadelphia it found available to it two sharply opposed conceptions of the executive rôle. That which had found embodiment in the great majority of the state constitutions was expressed by Sherman, of Connecticut, in the following words: "He considered the executive magistracy as nothing more than an institution for the carrying of the will of the legislature into effect," so that the person or persons upon whom it was devolved (and he favored a collegiate executive) "ought to be appointed by and accountable to the legislature only," "the depository of the supreme will of society."[56]

The leading exponents of the opposed conception were James Wilson and Gouverneur Morris.[57] Both urged that the executive should be a single person, elected by the people at large, capable of indefinite reëligibility, and vested with an absolute veto.[58] Furthermore, he should be recognized as inheriting a generous slice of the British royal prerogative, although not all of it, since the power of declaring war and entering into treaties involved elements of legislative power. For the rest, the effervescent and voluble Morris voiced his conception of the office as follows:

The executive magistrate should be the guardian of the people, even of the lower classes . . . against the great and the wealthy, who in the course of things will necessarily compose the legislative body. Wealth tends to corrupt the mind, to nourish its love of power, to stimulate it to oppression. History proves this to be the spirit of the opulent. . . . The Executive, therefore, ought to be so constituted as to be the great protector of the masses of the people.[59]

Being unable to foresee the industrial revolution, Morris was unable to foresee that "the great and the wealthy" might often find it more to their advantage to limit legislative authority with a view to securing the unobstructed direct application of their economic power rather than to exalt it as an instrument of indirect aggrandizement. But in its reading of human nature, his forecast shows great insight.

That the Wilson-Morris conception of executive power prevailed in much larger measure than the opposing view becomes at once apparent from a perusal of the Constitution itself. At one point, indeed, and that of first importance, the triumph of the strong executive view may not have been precisely intended by the Convention itself. Writing Pickering in 1814, Gouverneur Morris, who gave the Constitution its final form, said: "That instrument was written by the fingers which write this letter," and proceeded to avow that he had seized the opportunity "to select phrases, which expressing my own notions would not alarm others, nor shock their self-love."[60] He confined this avowal to the judicial power, but it seems clear that it might equally well have embraced the executive power. For in the form in which it was referred to the Committee on Style, what is today the opening clause of Article II merely settled the controversy whether there should be a plural or single executive. It read: "The executive power of the United States shall be vested in a single person. His stile shall be 'The President of the United

States of America'; his title shall be 'His Excellency.' "[61] Nor was the final form of the clause, "The Executive power shall be vested in the President of the United States," ever separately acted upon by the Convention. In such fortuitous fashion was our constitutional law bequeathed one of its most vital controversies—its *most* vital for the idea of "a government of laws and not of men"— that respecting the source and scope of Presidential power under the Constitution.

Is the opening clause of Article II a grant of power or merely a designation of office? The view that it is the former encounters the obvious objection that it renders some of the ensuing clauses of the same article superfluous. Despite which Chief Justice Taft's opinion for the Court in *Myers* v. *United States*, decided in 1926, unmistakably transmutes this view into constitutional law, thereby terminating a controversy which had been waged with varying fortunes for nearly 140 years.

Madison had started the ball of "executive power" rolling in the first Congress, and was so far successful that by the "decision of 1789" the power was conceded the President to remove certain high executive officers appointed by him "by and with the advice and consent of the Senate," without obtaining that consent. This, of course, is familiar history. There is, however, one feature of Madison's case for attributing to the President alone the removal power over executive officers which has been generally overlooked, and that is his further insistence that the President was entitled to *"control"* the conduct of his subordinates.[62]

This, moreover, was Jackson's position exactly regarding his removal of Secretary Duane from the Treasury in 1833. Jackson justified his act not on the ground that the removal power was itself an unconditional power, but on the quite different and much more formidable proposition that it was the appropriate sanction provided by the Constitution for his further and unconditional power to control his subordinates in all their official actions.[63] And Taney's contemporary explanation of his own order removing the deposits asserted the same idea. He justified his course as within the discretion which the law establishing the Bank had vested in the Secretary of the Treasury, and his compliance with the President's command as a duty owing to the Chief Executive—in short, *his* discretion was the *President's*.[64]

Webster at the time savagely attacked this theory of the President's relation to law enforcement as utterly irreconcilable with the idea of "a government of laws and not of men," and the Court in the Kendall Case went out of its way to visit a special censure upon it.[65] Chief Justice Taft, in his opinion in the Myers Case, nevertheless, ratifies the entire Jacksonian position, although at one point he endeavors to avoid one of its obvious consequences. "There may be," he writes, "duties of a quasi-judicial character imposed on executive officers and members of executive tribunals . . . the discharge of which the

President can not in a particular case properly influence or control." But he straightway adds: "Even in such a case he [the President] may consider the decision after its rendition as a reason for removing the officer" on the ground that the latter had not exercised his discretion wisely.[66] The qualification manifestly amounts to nothing; and unless the Court chooses to disavow the greater part of the Taft opinion, it will have to say so when it comes to pass upon Mr. Humphrey's recent removal from the Federal Trade Commission.[67] Meantime the New Deal, involving as it does vast delegations of power to the President, will have enhanced enormously the practical case for the Jackson-Taft thesis.

The doctrine, therefore, that the opening clause of Article II is a grant of power, and hence vests in the President the entire "executive power of the United States" (and not merely the items of executive power thereinafter specified), produces the further doctrine that there can be no discretionary power under the laws of Congress which does not belong to the President if he chooses to claim it. And, of course, the President can be held accountable only politically for his exercise of a discretion which is his legally and constitutionally. Furthermore, as we shall see presently, the whole tendency of legislation in recent years has been in the direction of leaving more and more to executive discretion—that is, to a legally uncontrollable Presidential discretion in the last analysis.

IV.

HOWEVER, before considering this aspect of "a government of laws and not of men" under modern conditions, I wish to discuss briefly a second corollary of the idea that the opening clause of Article II is the source of the President's power. As is pointed out by Chief Justice Marshall in *Marbury* v. *Madison*, the Constitution itself endows the President "with certain important political powers in the exercise of which he is to use his own discretion, and is accountable only to his country in his political character and to his own conscience."[68] What is the scope of such political powers? The question was raised for the first time by Hamilton in 1793, in his "Letters of Pacificus," which were written in defense of Washington's so-called "Proclamation of Neutrality" of that year. There is no mention of such a power in the body of Article II; but it was Hamilton's contention that there did not have to be, since the opening clause of the article conferred on the President the full "executive power of the United States." As Madison discerningly pointed out in his answering "Letters of Helvidius," what Hamilton's argument really amounted to was an attempt to infuse the expression "executive power" with the British royal prerogative.[69] But later doctrine and practice fully vindicate Hamilton's thesis; indeed, in one important respect they outrun it.

The reason why Locke, although a Whig, could give the royal prerogative such indefinite scope was that he attributed to Parliament the power to supply a corrective for all abuses of power by the monarch; and by the maxim "a government of laws and not of men," as originally conceived in this country, a similar recourse was open to the legislative powers of Congress. That is to say, the maxim at first implied the natural primacy of the legislative power over the executive and judicial branches, and a general directory power over them.[70] This idea Jackson totally rejected, and it is his most notable contribution to American constitutional law and theory. The President was one of three *equal* departments of government, each of which was entitled to select the occasions for the exercise of its respective constitutional powers without the aid or consent of either of the others and without any compulsion therefrom. This was the Jacksonian tenet.

Once again the Myers Case authenticates the triumph of the Jacksonian thesis. The Chief Justice there holds that because the removal power as respects executive officers resides in the President as a part of his "executive power," Congress may not in the creation of such offices qualify in any way the removability of their incumbents. Or, speaking in general terms, in a clash between the President and Congress, it is the former's power which should be defined first, and the resulting definition comprises an independent limitation upon Congressional power.

We are thus brought to still another aspect of "executive power" in relation to "a government of laws and not of men." Executive power is residual power—it is what is left of the original competence of government after the relatively specialized functions of legislation and adjudication have been subtracted therefrom. Also, it is usually concentrated in few hands, wields the physical forces of government, and presumably at least is prepared at all times for instant action.[71] It has, therefore, a special adaptability to unusual and peculiarly dangerous situations, of which war, or threat of war, has in the past furnished the supreme exemplification. On the other hand, if it is fair to demand of the executive that he be ready for sudden and unpredictable emergencies how can it also be demanded that he always keep within law that was devised for normal times?

The simplest answer is that this cannot be demanded. "The King," said Justice Vernon in Ship-Money Case, "*pro bono publico* may charge his subjects for the safety and defence of the kingdom, notwithstanding any act of Parliament . . . and the King may dispense with any law in cases of necessity."[72] As we saw above, the prerogative here claimed for the monarch in cases of necessity is expanded by Locke to reach cases of public convenience merely. To what extent, and with what results, have these views found lodgment in American constitutional theory?

One's starting point is naturally Lincoln's message of July 4, 1861, to Congress, where in so many words he lays claim to "the war power," partly on the ground of his "executive power" and partly as Commander in Chief;[73] nor did he ever abandon the idea that on the one ground or the other he possessed extraordinary resources of power which Congress lacked and the exercise of which it could not substantially control. Thus in justifying the Emancipation Proclamation he asserted broadly, "As Commander-in-Chief, I suppose I have a right to take any measure which may subdue the enemy." And again: "I felt that measures otherwise unconstitutional might become lawful by becoming indispensable to the preservation of the Constitution through the preservation of the nation."[74] That is to say, back of the Constitution stands the nation, endowed with a right to self-preservation whereof the Presidency is the constitutionally designated instrument.

When first confronted with this theory in the Prize Cases,[75] in the midst of war, the Court treated it with great indulgence, to say the least; but in *Ex parte Milligan*[76] it swung violently to the other direction, adopting the comfortable position that the normal powers of the government were perfectly adequate to any emergency that could possibly arise, and citing the war just "happily terminated" in proof! Indeed Justice Davis' opinion for the majority virtually ratifies Jeremiah Black's argument for Milligan, that "a violation of law on the pretence of saving such a government as ours is not self-preservation, but suicide"[77]—certainly the last word in constitutionalism!

The Court's vacillation is by no means inexplicable—even forgetting the fact that when it decided the Milligan Case it was no longer in daily peril of being bagged by some Confederate raider. As the majority opinions in the second Legal Tender Cases,[78] decided a few years later, strongly suggest, its hesitation was not so much over recognizing as inherent in the *nation* a power of self-preservation, as over the endeavor to articulate this power with the Constitution solely through the "executive power" and "Commander in Chief" clauses.[79] Certain it is that since then the Court has repeatedly attributed powers to the national government as a whole, and hence to Congress as their primary repository, simply on the ground of national necessity or on the ground that such powers corresponded to, and grew out of, acknowledged attributes of the American *nation* at international law.[80] The words of Justice Holmes in *Missouri* v. *Holland* summarize a doctrine the potentialities of which remain for the future to disclose: "It is not lightly to be assumed that in matters requiring national action, a power which must belong to and somewhere reside in every civilized government is not to be found."[81]

The question remains, however, whether the above recognition of an inherent power in the national government as a whole to deal with national emergencies enables us to expel the concept of "executive power" as residual power from this "government of laws and not of men." Certainly not altogether; at least if we do, we speedily discover that we have in effect to readmit the repudiated concept in a different guise. In this connection two facts are of special relevancy: first, that the President is *a single individual*, and, secondly, that he is *always on the job*. In the former quality he is not only natural heir to such ceremonious attributes of monarchy as the Republic may choose to tolerate, but he is the representative of the *unity* of the nation, whereas, as President Jackson was at pains to explain, Congress represents it only in pieces. Then always being on the job, he is always ready to do the thing that simply has to be done, and likewise is always ready to gather to himself any stray odds and ends of authority that may be looking for a convenient repository.

For instance, we find the Supreme Court at its first term ordering "that (unless and until it shall be otherwise provided by law) all process of this Court shall be in the name of 'the President of the United States' "[82]—and it never has been "otherwise provided by law." So also, it early became necessary to attribute to the United States certain corporate capacities, the right to sue and be sued, the right to enter into contracts, the right to ask the courts to cancel fraudulent contracts, and so on and so forth; and invariably the custodian of such capacities was held to be the executive department.[83]

Nor is the credit which should go in this connection to the successive occupants of the office of Attorney-General by any means slight. For many of these family lawyers of the Administration have labored in season and out to build up a strong conception of Presidential power. As early as 1831 we find an Attorney-General arguing before the Supreme Court that in performance of the trust enjoined upon him by the "faithful execution" clause, the President "not only may, but . . . is bound to avail himself of every appropriate means not forbidden by law."[84] Noteworthy, too, is a series of opinions handed down by Attorney-General Cushing in the course of the years 1853 to 1855. In one of these the Attorney-General laid down the doctrine that a marshal of the United States, when opposed in the execution of his duty by unlawful combinations too powerful to be dealt with by the ordinary processes of a federal court, had authority to summon the entire able-bodied force of his precinct as a *posse comitatus*, comprising not only bystanders and citizens generally but any and all armed forces,[85] which is precisely the theory upon which President Lincoln based his call for volunteers in April, 1861.

And in the famous Neagle Case,[86] decided in 1890, the Supreme Court not only ratified these doctrines—it distended them. Neagle, a United States marshal, having been jailed by the California authorities for killing one Terry, was asking to be released on writ of *habeas corpus*, his plea being that he had shot Terry in discharge of the duty to which he had been assigned by the Attorney-General of the United States, of protecting Justice Field, whose life Terry had threatened. It was not questioned that if Neagle had acted "in pursuance of a law of the United States" he was entitled to his discharge under section 753 of the Revised Statutes; but where was the law which could be invoked in his behalf? The Court held that the order of the Attorney-General to Neagle could be attributed to the President and hence had adequate basis in the latter's duty to "take care that the laws be faithfully executed." Said Justice Miller, the President's duty is not limited "to the enforcement of the acts of Congress or of treaties of the United States according to their express terms," but also embraces "the rights, duties and obligations growing out of the Constitution itself, our international relations, and all the protection implied by the nature of the government under the Constitution"; and then, as if this was not sufficiently broad doctrine, the Justice added the happy suggestion that there is "a peace of the United States"; that is, in effect, a peace of the President of the United States.[87]

Five years later, in the Debs Case,[88] the Court sustained the right of the national executive to go into the national courts and secure an injunction against striking railway employees who were interfering with interstate commerce, as well as to despatch troops against such strikers, although it was conceded in effect that there was no statutory basis for either action.[89] The case is interpreted by ex-President Taft as illustrating the idea advanced in the Neagle Case of "a peace of the United States" entitled to the peculiar protection of the President.[90]

The Neagle Case has, however, yet another interest than that which comes from its bringing to focus much previously rather loosely held opinion. It is also the immediate source of the first President Roosevelt's so-called "stewardship theory" of the Presidency. Endeavoring in his *Autobiography* to account for the great achievements of his administration, Mr. Roosevelt found them to be attributable in no small measure to his theory that the President's power, being that of "a steward of the people," "was limited only by specific restrictions and prohibitions appearing in the Constitution or imposed by Congress under its constitutional powers."[91] It would follow, of course, that if and when Congress lacked the constitutional power to do something in the public interest, its deficiency would become a mandate to the "executive power" to do it; nor, obviously, would executive action taken on this premise be subject to Congressional control. On the contrary, by the Myers Case it would, apparently, set a limit to Congressional action which were otherwise constitutional.

Thus compounded with the principle of the separation of powers, in substitution for the principle of legislative supremacy, the Lockian theory of executive prerogative becomes something closely akin to a prescription for dictatorship, and on this ground ex-President Taft vigorously assailed the Roosevelt thesis in his book entitled *Our Chief Magistrate and His Powers*. Protesting that the President has no constitutional warrant to attempt the rôle of "a universal providence," Mr.

Taft went on to state his own view thus: "The true view of the executive functions is, as I conceive it, that the President can exercise no power which cannot be fairly and reasonably traced to some specific grant or justly implied and included within such express grant as proper and necessary."[92] These words were written in 1916. Ten years later the author of them was spokesman for the Court in the Myers Case.

V.

TURNING then to the New Deal, what attitude may it be said to represent on this subject of dictatorship? The answer is, I think, that in this respect the New Deal is fairly assessed as *an effort to attain some of the results of dictatorship by a mergence of legislative power with Presidential leadership*—in the words of President Roosevelt, their "firm and permanent union." Which brings us again into contact with the concept of "legislative power" in "a government of laws and not of men," but first of all with another famous maxim of American constitutional theory.

In the Digest of Justinian occurs the precept that "one vested with a jurisdiction may not confer it on another," the reference being apparently to the power of judging. A medieval gloss on this text states its import in the phrase "*delegatus non potest delegare*." Still later, Bracton, writing in the thirteenth century with the problem of subinfeudation in mind, with which the statute of *Quia*

Emptores was presently to deal, wrote: "*Jurisdic-tio delegata non delegari potest*"; and it was from this source in all probability that Coke, with his flair for the Latin tag wherewith to furnish out his own ideas with a glamorous antiquity, obtained the phrase "*delegata potestas non potest delegari.*"[93] The reference is still to *jurisdiction;* and the thought evidently is that, this being a matter of trust reposed in men of special learning and capacity, must be exercised personally and not by deputy.

The form, however, in which the maxim is of interest to us comes from Locke's *Treatise on Civil Government.* These are his words: "The legislature cannot transfer the power of making laws to any other hands, for it being but a delegated power from the people, they who have it cannot pass it over to others."[94] What precisely did Locke mean by these words? One thing certainly he did not mean, and that is that all discretionary power in the state should be confined to the legislative body. On the contrary, as we have seen, he gave the royal prerogative the broadest dimensions. But he did this in reliance on the ultimate supremacy of Parliament, that is, of the legislative power. Thus, if this broad and superabundant royal prerogative was to be adequately controlled, one thing must be assured, namely, that Parliament should not abdicate its power.

In other words, the problem with which Locke was struggling was to preserve the historic constitution of the English realm, centering about the royal prerogative as its active element, and at the same time to secure the grand result of the Glorious Revolution just completed, namely, Parliamentary supremacy. And as further indicating Locke's intention we should recall the actual precariousness of Parliamentary control even after the Revolution. Parliament still met only on summons by the King (as is, indeed, the case today); could be prorogued or dissolved by the King at will; and the royal veto was still active and absolute. The absorption of both prerogative and the legislative power by the Cabinet was a solution which Locke could not possibly have foreseen.

The transplantation of Locke's doctrine to this country was due to two things. First of these was the logic of the principle of the separation of powers—for why go to the trouble of separating the legislative and executive power if they could still remerge at any time of their own motion? Secondly, it was due to the profound distrust manifested in the early state constitutions of "the executive magistracy," to use Madison's words. But with these considerations in mind, the maxim takes on a very different significance from what it has in Locke's pages. The theory that now emerges is that the *discretionary* power of the state is lodged in the legislature alone and must remain there, while executive power is purely *ministerial* in nature and must be kept so. Statutes, therefore, must be couched in definite terms, leaving almost nothing to the judgment or discretion of the law-enforcing bodies, whether executive or judicial.

But obviously a government whose action was clogged by such a doctrine could act only in relatively simple and stereotyped situations, situations previsible in detail by the legislative body. For a complex and changing society, the maxim, in its very solicitude for the legislative authority, strangulates and destroys that authority! And by the same token, this maxim confronts such a society with the alternative of minimizing governmental control to the utmost or else of falling back upon the primitive conception of executive power; or, what is more probable, it invites the latter recourse as the ultimate escape from the former.

The actual effect of the maxim as a constitutional restraint upon American legislative power has nevertheless been slight, although the story is not without its instructive features. Prior to the Civil War the principal application of the maxim occurred in the later Forties, when in a few states it was invoked to invalidate local-opinion laws prohibitive of the liquor traffic.[95] Forty years later the advocates and beneficiaries of *laissez faire* seized upon the maxim as forbidding the efforts of the state legislature to delegate the acknowledged "legislative power" of rate regulation to the first railway commissions. In the leading case of *State v. Chicago, Milwaukee and St. Paul Railway Company*, the Minnesota Supreme Court met and disposed of this contention with the simple statement that "if such a power is to be exercised at all, it can only be satisfactorily done by a board or commission."[96] In other words, whether the legislature should delegate its powers or not was largely a matter of convenience.

Nor can it be seriously questioned that this is approximately the doctrine which the Supreme Court today applies to Congressional delegations of power. In *Buttfield* v. *Stranahan*[97] the question at issue was the validity of a measure whereby Congress had directed the Secretary of the Treasury to establish uniform standards of quality for tea to be imported into the United States. Said Justice White, speaking for the Court:

Congress legislated on the subject as far as was reasonably practicable, and from the necessities of the case was compelled to leave to executive officials the duty of bringing about the result pointed out by the statute. To deny the power of Congress to delegate such a duty would, in effect, amount to declaring that the plenary power vested in Congress to regulate foreign commerce could not be efficaciously exercised.[98]

And in *Clark Distilling Co.* v. *West Maryland R.R.*,[99] the same Justice, again speaking for the Court, met the contention that the Webb-Kenyon Act unconstitutionally delegated Congress' power to regulate interestate commerce to the states by pointing out that Congress could recover such power as it had delegated at any time.[100] What the maxim, as thus applied, amounts to is little if anything more than the truism that a legislature cannot diminish the powers of its successors—that, in other words, legislative power is not lessened by its exercise. It thus becomes assimilated to the "neces-

sary and proper" clause, and Congress is enabled
to delegate its powers whenever it is necessary and
proper to do so in order to exercise them effectively. Extensive, therefore, as is the power which
the New Deal legislation delegates the President, it
in this regard only confirms the uncontradicted
trend for years past of our constitutional law.

Yet it is evident that the maxim lent itself very
logically to the concept of "a government of laws
and not of men," which presupposes that any
situation, in order to be brought under governmental control, should first receive definition in a
nearly automatic rule of law. With present-day
conditions such a theory is evidently out of touch.
The only question, therefore, is whether the necessarily augmented powers of government shall continue to find expression and modulation through
statutory rules announced beforehand, albeit in
broad and flexible terms. The minimization of the
taboo upon delegated legislative power, sketched
above, by keeping legislation a still feasible technique of government, answers this question in the
affirmative.

The final aspect of "a government of laws and
not of men," as it is conceived in the American
constitutional system, may be dismissed very
briefly. I refer to judicial review of delegated legislation. In this field the Court has today a wide
choice among formulas, but the very necessity
which calls for delegated legislation must, if it per-
sists, gradually restrict choice to those doctrines
which confine the Court's supervisory rôle to com-

paratively modest dimensions.[101] If legislative prevision of the future is impracticable, judicial prevision of it can hardly be more so. The history of
the Interstate Commerce Commission gives assurance, moreover, that the judiciary will respond to
a determined and consistently prosecuted legislative policy. Hence, as judicial review comes less
and less to be justified on *laissez faire* premises,
the Court, it may be predicted, will recognize more
and more readily that power delegated to an administrative body should be exercised in accordance with the type of discretion which such a body
exercises, not in accordance with judicial discretion.[102]

To summarize: From legal history emerge two
conceptions of law—that of a code of intrinsic
justice, not of human creation but discoverable by
human reason, and that of a body of ordinances
assertive of human will and owing its binding force
thereto. The idea of a "government of laws and
not of men" originally predicated the sway of
the former kind of law and a "legislative power"
which was merely a power to declare such law, and
hence was indistinguishable in principle from "judicial power." But as we saw in the previous chapter, the very essence of the American conception of
the separation of powers is its insistence upon the
inherent distinction between law-making and law-
interpreting, and its assignment of the latter to
the judiciary, a notion which, when brought to
bear upon the Constitution, yields judicial review.

For all that, the idea that legislative power embraces an element of law-declaring power has never been entirely expelled from our inherited legal traditions, while, conversely, modern analysis of the interpretative function exercised by courts plainly discloses that it involves unavoidably an exercise of choice substantially legislative in character; and especially is this so as to the Supreme Court's interpretations of the national Constitution, on account of the wealth of alternative doctrines from which the Court may at any time approach its task of interpretation. In short, the meaning of "a government of laws" in our constitutional law and theory is government subject to judicial disallowance.

On the other hand, the working theory of the national Constitution has embraced from the first, and with about equal fervency, both of the antinomies inferred in Harrington's formula; while the Supreme Court, pursuing still the ancient grudge against "legislative power" in which judicial review was first conceived, has steadily favored the aggrandizement of the "executive power" of the President. The net result is that our constitutional law and theory today ascribes to the President an indefinite range of "inherent" powers, places these beyond the reach of Congressional curtailment, enables the President to receive and exercise delegated legislative powers of indefinite range, and attributes to him alone all nonjudicial discretion which either the Constitution or the laws of Congress permit.

So leaving the New Deal entirely out of the question "a government of laws and not of men" appears today to be in a state somewhat akin to that of dual federalism, thanks in part to the distinguished labors of James Madison, Alexander Hamilton, Andrew Jackson, Abraham Lincoln, and Theodore Roosevelt; and thanks further to the Supreme Court's ratification of these labors and its transmutation of them into law of the Constitution. Indeed, it would seem that the New Deal ought to be considered as bringing support and encouragement to the cause of "a government of laws and not of men" rather than otherwise, inasmuch as whatever claims to power it represents are advanced on behalf of the national government as *a whole*, and hence have first to run the legislative gantlet. In brief, *the New Deal envisages the legislative authority as the supreme authority of government*; and endeavors to adapt this authority to modern conditions, first, by associating with it Presidential leadership and, secondly, by confining its action to the larger questions of principle, leaving lesser issues to the more flexible methods of administration. Dictatorship or the avoidance of it is hardly a matter which will be settled by the precedents and doctrines of constitutional law and theory. Still it can be said with some assurance that the latter outcome would not be aided by denying to the national government as a whole powers which correspond to the actual unity of the country and which predicate its single destiny.[103]

CHAPTER IV

THE BREAKDOWN OF CONSTITUTIONAL LIMITATIONS—THE SPENDING POWER

I.

A RECENT issue of that popular literary and political miscellany known as the *Congressional Record* contained the following quaint item:

I return without my approval House bill no. 10203, an act to enable the Commissioner of Agriculture to make a special distribution of seed in the drought-stricken counties of Texas and making an appropriation therefor.

It is represented that a long-continued and extensive drought has existed in certain portions of the State of Texas resulting in a failure of crops and consequent distress and destitution. Yet I feel obliged to withhold my approval of the plan, as proposed by this bill, to indulge a benevolent and charitable sentiment through the appropriation of public funds for that purpose.

I can find no warrant for such an appropriation in the Constitution and I do not believe that the power and duty of the General Government ought to be extended to the relief of individual suffering which is in no manner properly related to the public service or benefit.[1]

The author of this brief essay on constitutional ethics was the late President Cleveland, and its date the year 1887. The appropriation which the vetoed measure carried was $10,000; and the total

expenditure of the national government for that
year was somewhat less than 268 millions.

Forty-seven years later, on January 4, 1934, to
be precise, the President of the United States laid
before the House a budget calling for an expenditure of $10,569,000,000 for the current fiscal
year, of which four billions were intended for
private relief through loans to various enterprises,
while still another billion was to finance direct relief or loans and grants to states and municipali-
ties—some of them for the payment of teachers'
salaries. Nira herself is a very freehanded young
woman, having had at her disposal originally some
three billion, three hundred millions for public
works, of which nearly fifty millions have been or
will be devoted to social and economic experimentation in the Tennessee Valley—a sort of amalga-
mation, Mr. Arthur Krock, of the *New York
Times* opines, of Brook Farm, the Aurora Colony,
Dnieprostroy, Schenectady and Martin Chuzzle-
wit's Eden. Cheap power, model communities,
large-scale zoning, soil erosion checks, reforestry,
and flood control—this is but a partial list of the
objectives avowed by those who are directing this
unique experiment.

Nor is it altogether surprising to discover that
this liberality on the part of the national government has met a receptive attitude on the part of
the local governmental agencies on whose coöperation the national relief program in some measure
depends. Two days prior to President Roosevelt's
Budget Message, Governor Lehman of New York

addressed over the radio the National Housing Conference. To his nation-wide audience the governor of the premier state of the Union said:

In the State of New York today there exist conditions of housing which are a menace to the health and general well-being of our citizens obliged to live under them. . . .

Previous to the existing crisis the majority of the people of our State have held the attitude that housing was a matter of individual responsibility. . . .

Rather suddenly, a whole new set of attitudes has swept even the more conservative sections of the community into a willingness to accept as a joint responsibility the obligation to provide good housing for the lower income groups. . . .

Already housing commissions have been created in Detroit, Cleveland, Los Angeles, Cincinnati, Milwaukee and Toledo. Many other communities will soon follow. It is my earnest hope that the people of New York will be in the vanguard in this movement to promote recovery by means of slum clearance and low-cost housing.

This tells the essential story. Our ten-billion-dollar budget is the first fruit to come to maturity of an altered outlook upon governmental function. So again the question arises of how this altered outlook, thus expressed in terms of dollars and cents, accords with the conventional pattern of American constitutional law and theory. This time, however, we find ourselves confronted with a quite different body of evidence than before. In the field of expenditure Congress and the President, the national legislative authority, has read the Constitution for itself, has set its own limits;

and the results of judicial review, while not in all respects negligible, have not crystallized as judicially enforcible limitations on national power.

Article I, Section 8, Clause 1, of the Constitution reads as follows: "The Congress shall have power to lay and collect taxes, duties, imposts, and excises, to pay the debts and provide for the common defense and general welfare of the United States; but all duties, imposts, and excises shall be uniform throughout the United States."[2] The phrase which demands special scrutiny is that which authorizes Congress to "provide," in some way or other, "for the general welfare." Our inquiry is accordingly twofold: by what *means* precisely may Congress "provide" for the general welfare; and what *is* the "general welfare" for which it may provide? The first question may be disposed of rather briefly; but the second involves an extensive examination into Congressional and Presidential opinion and action.

While adoption of the Constitution was pending some of its opponents made the charge that the phrase "to provide for the general welfare" was a sort of legislative joker which was designed, in conjunction with the "necessary and proper" clause, to vest Congress with power to provide for whatever it might choose to regard as the "general welfare" by any means deemed by it to be "necessary and proper."[3] The suggestion was promptly repudiated by advocates of the Constitution[4] on the following grounds. In the first place, it was pointed out, the phrase stood between two other phrases, both dealing with the taxing power—an awkward syntax on the assumption under consideration. In the second place, the phrase was coördinate with the phrase "to pay the debts," that is, a purpose of money expenditure only. Finally, it was asserted, the suggested reading, by endowing Congress with practically complete legislative power, rendered the succeeding enumeration of more specific powers superfluous, thereby reducing "the Constitution to a single phrase."

In the total this argument sounds impressive, but on closer examination it becomes less so, especially today. For one thing, it is a fact that in certain early printings of the Constitution the "common defense and general welfare" clause appears separately paragraphed, while in others it is set off from the "lay and collect" clause by a semicolon and not, as modern usage would require, by the less awesome comma.[5] To be sure, the semicolon may have been due in the first instance to the splattering of a goose quill that needed trimming, for it is notorious that the fate of nations has often turned on just such minute *points*.

Then as to the third argument—while once deemed an extremely weighty one—it cannot be so regarded in light of the decision in 1926 in the case of *Myers* v. *United States*. As I mentioned in the previous chapter, the Court held on that occasion that the opening clause of Article II of the Constitution which says that "the executive power shall be vested in a President of the United States," is not a simple designation of office but a grant of power, which the succeeding clauses of the same article either qualify or to which they lend "appropriate emphasis."[6] Granting the soundness of this position, however, why should not the more specific clauses of Article I be regarded as standing in a like relation to the "general welfare" clause thereof? Nor is this by any means all that may be said in favor of treating the latter clause as a grant of substantive legislative power, as anyone may convince himself who chooses to consult Mr. James Francis Lawson's minute and ingenious examination of the subject.[7]

II.

ASSUMING, nevertheless, that it is only by *spending* that the national legislative power may constitutionally provide for "the general welfare," the question still remains, what is that "general welfare" which Congress may thus promote? It is a case where the most *literal* meaning of words is also their most *liberal* meaning, and in *Federalist 30* and *34* we find Hamilton assigning them this significance; while on the other hand we find Madison parting company from his associate along characteristic lines. In harmony with his thesis of dual federalism, Madison, in *Federalist 41*, confines the "general welfare" which Congress may promote by taxation and expenditure to that welfare which it may promote by its other delegated powers. The spending power, in short, is *instrumental*; the clause which confers it, a second "co-efficient" clause.[8]

The difficulty in the way of Madison's view, which, by its author's own admission, detracts from the literal meaning of words, has never been better pointed out than by Story in his *Commentaries:*

If there are no other cases which can concern the common defence and general welfare except those within the scope of the enumerated powers, the discussion is merely nominal and frivolous. If there are such cases, who is at liberty to say, that being for the common defence and general welfare, the Constitution did not intend to embrace them?[9]

But Madison had also urged in support of his theory the fact that the phrase "common defense and general welfare" was taken from the Articles of Confederation, the suggestion being that it could not have been the intention of an instrument which so carefully safeguarded the "sovereignty" of the states, to vest Congress with an indefinite power of appropriation. Yet he himself was forced to admit that, even after the adoption of the Articles, "habit and a continued expediency, amounting often to a real or apparent necessity, prolonged the exercise of an undefined authority" in this as well as in some other respects.[10] Thus, given simply their literal force, the phraseology of the Articles of Confederation dealing with the power of expenditure did in fact represent the actual practice of Congress prior to the Constitution.

The classic statement of the literal—and liberal

—view of the "general welfare" clause occurs in Hamilton's Report on Manufactures, in 1791.[11] The relevant part of this famous document reads as follows:

The phrase is as comprehensive as any that could have been used, because it was not fit that the constitutional authority of the Union to appropriate its revenues should have been restricted within narrower limits than the "general welfare," and because this necessarily embraces a vast variety of particulars which are susceptible neither of specification nor of definition. It is therefore of necessity left to the discretion of the National Legislature to pronounce upon the objects which concern the general welfare, and for which, under that description, an appropriation of money is requisite and proper. And there seems to be no room for a doubt that whatever concerns the general interests of learning, of agriculture, of manufactures, and of commerce, are within the sphere of the national councils, *as far as regards an application of money.*[12]

The practical nub of Hamilton's argument was a system of bounties for selected lines of manufacture; and though it otherwise bore no fruit, it may have furnished one reason why Congress voted the following February a subsidy to the cod fisheries, a proposal against which Madison vainly urged his narrow doctrine of the power of expenditure.[13] Nearly five years later, Washington, in his final message to Congress, brought forward a series of recommendations implying the possession by Congress of the broadest discretion in expenditure: manufactures on public account, encouragement of agriculture, a national university—none of which, obviously, can be vindicated except by reference to the "general welfare" clause.[14] Worth noting, too, is Madison's complaint that the report of a committee of Congress, January, 1797, which supported the President's recommendations in behalf of agriculture, received not "the slightest mark of disapprobation from the authorities to which it was addressed."[15]

A few months later, in the Virginia and Kentucky Resolutions, was promulgated the theory that the Constitution reserved to the states a mediating function between the people and the national government. It followed that the national government, before undertaking within the boundaries of the states any new or unaccustomed activity, must secure their consent. Indeed, it came to be insisted that the "necessary and proper" clause implied this requirement, since no matter how *necessary* a measure might be as a means to a constitutional end, *propriety* required that the state or states immediately concerned should be consulted; and this doctrine was felt to be especially applicable to the construction by the national government of public works within the states on account of the likelihood that national expenditures would carry with them jurisdictional consequences.[16]

Then in 1802 the famous Cumberland Road, to run from a point in Maryland to Ohio, was authorized by Congress. The act specified various features of the construction and stipulated that the consent of the states affected should be obtained. All these acts received Jefferson's approval; as also, presumably, did Gallatin's ambitious project in 1808, which called for a great canal from north to south along the Atlantic Coast and a vast system of interior communications between the Atlantic on the one hand and the Great Lakes and Western rivers on the other. Though the scheme as a whole proved abortive, the national government opened between the years 1806 and 1817 some eleven roads in various parts of the country, most of them log roads to be sure, but good constitutional precedents for all that.[17]

Meantime, in December, 1816, there had been introduced into Congress a measure which called for the segregation of the "bonus" from the recently chartered National Bank, together with the government's share of the Bank's dividends, as a permanent fund pledged to internal improvements. This was the celebrated "Bonus Bill," and its sponsor was John C. Calhoun, at this stage a thoroughgoing nationalist. Defending the measure in the House, Calhoun recited two objections of a constitutional nature: "First, that they were to cut a road or canal through a state without its consent; and next that the public moneys can only be appropriated to effect the particular powers enumerated by the Constitution." The first objection he dismissed as not worth discussing, "since the good sense of the states might be relied on." Indeed, the thing to be feared was "in a different direction; in a too great solicitude to obtain an undue share to be expended within their respective limits." As to the second point, granting the objection by way of argument, he cited the "postal" clause and asked if it was not self-evident that the power "to establish post-roads" comprehended much more than the power merely to designate them. But his chief reliance was on the "general welfare" clause:

He was no advocate for refined arguments on the Constitution. The instrument was not intended as a thesis for a logician to exercise his ingenuity on. It ought to be construed with plain good sense. . . . If the framers had intended to limit the use of money to the powers afterwards enumerated and defined, nothing could be more easy than to have expressed it plainly.[18]

Although Madison had throughout the entire course of his administration permitted repeated infractions by Congress of the strict constitutional doctrine which he had developed in the *Federalist* with respect to Congress' spending power, the far-reaching scheme of the Bonus Bill seems to have revived his original scruples in all their intensity, and on his last day in office he returned the measure with his disapproval.[19] Monroe, moreover, in his first message to Congress, took occasion to serve notice that he shared the constitutional scruples of his predecessor and meant to govern himself accordingly unless the difficulty were met by constitutional amendment, a course which he urged.[20] In the main, nevertheless, the broader view remained as vital as ever. The passage in Monroe's message which was just alluded to was referred to a special committee of the House, headed by Tucker of Virginia, and on December 15 this committee reported.[21] It rejected the Presidential version of the Constitution on all points and even appeared to scout the doctrine of state consent. Whether by virtue of the "postal" clause, or the "commerce" clause, or by virtue of its military powers, the national government, the report asserted, had the right to construct and improve roads and cut canals, "at least with the consent of the states" affected. Passing then to the "general welfare" clause, the report continued: "It would be difficult to reconcile either the generality of the expression or the course of administration under it with the idea that Congress has not a discretionary power over its expenditures, limited only by their application to the common defense and the general welfare." As instances of past expenditures outside the range of the enumerated powers of Congress, the report mentioned the purchase of a library by the national government, of paintings, of the services of a chaplain, "liberal donations to the wretched sufferers of Venezuela," the despatch of the Lewis and Clarke expedition to the Pacific, the granting of bounties for the encouragement of the fisheries, and the "virtual bounties" which a protective tariff affords manufactures. Nor was it to be apprehended that this power would be abused "while the vigor of representative responsibility remains unimpaired. It is on this principle," the report continued, "that the framers of the Constitution mainly relied for the protection of the public purse. It was a safe reliance. It was manifest that there was no other subject on which representative responsibility would be so great." Furthermore, it was a case in which legislative discretion was absolutely necessary,

since no human foresight could discern, nor human industry enumerate the infinite varieties of purposes to which the public money might advantageously and legitimately be applied. The attempt would have been to *legislate,* not frame a constitution; to foresee and provide specifically for the wants of future generations, not to frame a rule of conduct for the legislative body.

At one point, however, the report does, inferentially at least, concede something to Madison's apprehensions. For it insists throughout that states always "retain their jurisdictional rights," whatever operations the national government might undertake within their limits, and whether with or without state consent. Unfortunately, the ground on which this confident assertion was rested is not disclosed by the committee.

The report soon produced fruit, for in the elaborate paper, entitled "Views of the President of the United States on the Subject of Internal Improvements,"[22] which he transmitted to the House of Representatives May 4, 1822, along with his veto of a bill "for the Preservation and Repair of the Cumberland Road," Monroe confessed that on the simple question of the right of Congress to raise and spend money he had undergone a complete change of views. "It was impossible to have

created," said he, "a power within the government
or any other power distinct from Congress and the
Executive which should control the movement of
the government in this respect and not destroy it.
Had it been declared by a clause in the Constitution that the expenditures under this grant should
be restricted to the construction which might be
given of the other grants, such restraint, though
the most innocent, could not have failed to have
had injurious effect on the vital principles of the
government and often on its most important measures." It followed that, while "each of the other
grants is limited by the nature of the grant itself,"
this is limited "by the nature of the government
only"—a qualification which is not elucidated. Nor
can there be any doubt that "good roads and
canals will promote many very important national
purposes." Likewise, there was the plain verdict of
the practice of the government from the beginning: "A practical construction, thus supported,
shows that it has reason on its side and is called for
by the interests of the Union. Hence, too, the presumption that it will be persevered in." And,
"wherein," he asked, "consists the danger of a liberal construction to the right of Congress to raise
and appropriate the public money? . . . Is not
the responsibility of the representative to his constituents in every branch of the general government equally strong, and as sensibly felt as in the
state governments, and is not the security against
abuse as effective in the one as in the other government?" In short, "My idea is that Congress has

an unlimited power to raise money, and that in its appropriation they have a discretionary power, restricted only by the duty to appropriate it to purposes of common defense and of general, not local, national not state benefit."

But the power of appropriation was one thing, jurisdiction quite another, and the former, Monroe insisted throughout, did not infer the latter. In his own words:

The right of appropriation is nothing more than a right to apply the public money to this or that purpose. It has no incidental power, nor does it draw after it any consequence of that kind. All that Congress could do under it in the case of internal improvements would be to appropriate the money necessary to make them. For every act requiring legislative sanction or support the State authority must be relied on. The condemnation of the land, if the proprietors should refuse to sell it, the establishment of turnpikes and tolls, and the protection of the work when finished must be done by the State. To these purposes the powers of the General Government are believed to be utterly incompetent.[23]

Supplemented by "repeated, liberal, and candid discussions in the Legislature," the "Views" "conciliated the sentiments and approximated the opinions of enlightened minds upon the question of constitutional power" for some years. On March 3, 1823, the first Rivers and Harbors Bill became law; in April of the following year $30,000 was appropriated for the survey of such roads and canals as the President should deem to be of national importance; by the act of March 3, 1825, was authorized a subscription of $300,000 to the stock of the Delaware and Chesapeake Canal; at the same session $200,000, together with a grant of 24,000 acres of land, was voted General Lafayette, then the country's guest. In his Inaugural the younger Adams sought to fire the imagination of Congress by citing "the magnificance and splendor" of the public works "of the ancient republics."[24] In his first message[25] he announced that surveys had been completed "for ascertaining the practicability of a canal from Chesapeake Bay to the Ohio River," for a road from Washington to New Orleans and for the union of the "waters of Lake Memphremagog with the Connecticut River"; also that surveys for roads in the territories of Florida, Arkansas, and Michigan and from Missouri to Mexico, as well as for the continuance of the Cumberland Road, were under way or had been completed. Even so, "the great object of the institution of civil government," "the improvement of those who are parties to the social compact," was not to be accomplished by roads and canals; "moral, political and intellectual improvements are duties assigned by the Author of Our Existence to social no less than to individual man," wherefore "governments are invested with power," the exercise of which for "the progressive improvement of the governed" "is a duty as sacred and indispensable as the usurpation of powers not granted is criminal and odious." Specifically, Adams, recurring to Washington's suggestion, urged a national university, national patronage of

voyages of discovery, the erection of an astronomi-
cal observatory. "There are," he noted, "one hundred and thirty of these light-houses of the skies"
scattered throughout Europe, "while throughout
the American hemisphere there is not one." He
also pressed the execution of the resolution of December 24, 1799, providing for a monument in the
city of Washington to the Father of his Country.
Nor did he doubt that the various powers of Congress were adequate to these objects; and if they
were, not to utilize them "would be treachery to
the most sacred of trusts." "The spirit of improvement," he concluded, "is abroad upon the earth."
"While foreign nations less blessed with that freedom which is power than ourselves are advancing
with gigantic strides in the career of public improvement, were we to slumber in indolence or fold
up our arms and proclaim to the world that we are
palsied by the will of our constituents, would it not
be to cast away the bounties of Providence and
doom ourselves to perpetual inferiority?"

Adams' vision outran the inclination of the
country, perhaps its resources; certainly it made
small appeal to the narrow imagination of the
frontiersman who came after him. Nevertheless, it
does not appear that Jackson ever formally rejected the doctrine which Monroe had developed as
to Congress' power in the appropriation of money;
on the contrary we find him attempting to foist
this doctrine on Madison as well, whose veto of the
Bonus Bill he interpreted, quite erroneously, as "a
concession that the right of appropriation is not

limited by the power to carry into effect the measures for which money is asked." At the same time, he is very explicit that no rights of jurisdiction ever accompany such appropriations, and also that they must be for "general not local, national not state" purposes. His emphasis on this latter point, both in his celebrated veto of the Maysville Road Bill on May 27, 1830,[26] and in later communications, constitutes in fact Jackson's individual contribution to the question of Congress' spending power; while the series of vetoes, based partly on this ground and partly on the ground that there ought to be no expenditures without attendant jurisdiction, by bringing to an abrupt close all large schemes of improvement by the national government, marks an epoch in the history of the subject. Pointing out in his message of December 1, 1834, that at the time of the veto of the Maysville Road Bill there had been reported to Congress bills calling for the appropriation of $106,000,-000 for internal improvements, while memorials before Congress called for projects which would have involved an expenditure of another hundred million, Jackson congratulated himself and the country upon his decisive stand on that occasion: "So far, at least, as it regards this branch of the subject, my best hopes have been realized. Nearly four years have elapsed and several sessions of Congress have intervened, and no attempt within my recollection has been made to induce Congress to exercise this power."[27]

From 1830 until the Civil War the constitutional controversy was transferred in the main from the broader issue of internal improvements to the narrower one of rivers and harbors bills, the first of which, as above noted, was signed by Monroe in 1823. The line of precedents for such measures, however, reaches back to the act of August 7, 1789, for the establishment and support of lighthouses, buoys, and other aids to navigation. Jackson, in an effort to apply his principle that appropriations must be for general, not local, purposes, wished to confine grants for rivers and harbors "to places below the ports of entry or delivery established by law,"[28] a test which speedily resulted in the creation by Congress of many new ports of entry. Tyler fell back on the Madisonian doctrine, while Polk, confronted in 1846 with a bill which appropriated $1,378,450, "to more than forty distinct and separate objects of improvement," urged that such works should be accomplished by the states, which should then recoup themselves from tonnage dues. Taylor and Fillmore, as loyal disciples of Clay, instigated rivers and harbors appropriations; Pierce reverted once more to the Madisonian position.[29]

So as we approach the Civil War we discover it to be the tendency of *Presidential* doctrine at least to return to the grounds of Madison's veto of 1817, enlarged however by an invocation of the "war power" in favor of a railway to the Pacific, a project which had been first suggested by the outcome of the Mexican War. Both Pierce and Buchanan recommended this enterprise by reference

to military necessity,[30] an argument which the out-
break of the Civil War rendered conclusive.

Nevertheless, it would be a mistake to suppose
that Congress' broader power of appropriation, in
however bad repute theoretically, was in fact defunct, even during that period when doctrines of
strict construction were dominant. In 1817 a committee of Congress had reported in favor of the
establishment of a Bureau of Agriculture, but the
suggestion had, like Washington's similar proposal, fallen by the wayside. Twenty-one years
later an appropriation for the "collection of agricultural statistics and other . . . agricultural purposes" was passed, and fourteen years after that
the purchase and distribution of seeds, which had
in fact begun as early as 1836, was specifically
provided for. Meantime, in 1850, an appropriation of $1,000 was made for the chemical analysis
of vegetable substances, and eight years after that
$3,500 was voted for the publication of informa-
tion concerning the consumption of cotton. The
Department of Agriculture itself was established
in 1862, and the year following $80,000 was voted
to its use, for the study of plant and animal diseases
and insect pests, of the culture of tobacco, silk
and cotton, irrigation, the adulteration of foods,
and the like.[31] The multifarious activities of this
department today, involving normally the annual
expenditure of tens of millions, are of common
knowledge. Yet this expansion seems to have
stirred little, if any, protest on constitutional
grounds, a remark which applies equally to the

parallel development of the Census, to the establishment of the Geological and Geodetic Surveys, to the creation of the Fisheries Bureau, the Bureau of Mines, and the Labor Bureau (now the Department of Labor), and to the participation of the government in the business of irrigation, game preservation, and so forth.

III.

THE final chapter in the growth of national expenditure prior to the Depression centers about the national government's entrance into the field of education. This began with the provision in the act under which Ohio was admitted to the Union in 1802—a provision harking back, in turn, to the Ordinance of 1787, indeed to the Ordinance of 1784, of which Jefferson was the principal author —whereby, in return for a grant of lands to each township in the state for public schools, and other concessions, the state pledged itself to refrain from taxing for a term of years lands sold by the national government to settlers. Later similar compacts were entered into with other states as they were admitted to the Union. Building upon these beginnings, and animated especially by its increasing interest in agricultural development, Congress in February, 1859, passed a bill the purpose of which was stated to be

the endowment, support and maintenance of at least one college [in each state] where the leading object shall be, without excluding other scientific or classical studies, to teach such branches of learning as are related to agriculture and the mechanic arts, as the legislatures of the states may respectively prescribe, in order to promote the liberal and practical education of the industrial classes in the several pursuits and professions of life.[32]

The bill assigned to each state twenty thousand acres of land for each Senator and Representative in the existing Congress and an additional twenty thousand for each Representative to which it might become entitled under the census of 1860. In return each state was required to "provide within five years . . . not less than one college, or the grant to said state" was to cease forthwith, and the state was to pay over to the United States any amounts it had received from lands previously sold. Other conditions also were specified, and the consent of the state must be communicated to the national government within two years.

The bill was upset by Presidential veto. Speaking to the constitutional issue, Buchanan wrote: "I presume the general proposition is undeniable that Congress does not possess the power to appropriate money in the Treasury, raised by taxes out of the people of the United States, for the purpose of educating the people of the respective states."[33] Any other view would mean "an actual consolidation of the federal and state governments so far as the great taxing and money power is concerned, and constitute a government of partnership between the two in the Treasury of the United States, equally ruinous to both." To be sure, he continued, the bill before him was justified as an exercise by Congress of its power "to dispose . . . of the territory and other property of the United States," but the argument was unacceptable: "The natural intendment would be that as the Constitution confined Congress to well defined specific powers, the funds placed at their command, whether in land or money, should be appropriated to the performance of the duties corresponding with these powers. If not, a government has been created with all its other powers carefully limited, but without any limitation in respect to the public lands."

Three years later the Morrill Act, embodying substantially the provisions which Buchanan had vetoed, but increasing the donation of lands for each Representative in Congress from twenty to thirty thousand acres, became law.[34] An amendment in 1866 extended its benefits to newly admitted states, and today there is probably not a state in the Union which has not long since accepted it. The Bureau of Education was created in the Department of the Interior in 1867, in part no doubt as an outcome of the Freedmen's Bureau. In 1870 we find President Grant urging an appropriation of proceeds from the sale of public lands to educational purposes, a recommendation which was renewed by his immediate successors,[35] and led finally to the enactment of the act of 1890. By this statute donations amounting eventually to $25,-000 per annum were to be made to each state and territory "for the more complete endowment and maintenance of colleges for the benefit of agricul-

ture and the mechanic arts" already established or
to be established in accordance with the Morrill
Act. The grant was made subject to certain conditions designed to secure equitable participation by
colored students in its benefits and to the legislative assent of the several states and territories.[36]

Thus was the transition effected from donations
of land to donations of money, though the latter
were still confined to proceeds from land sales.
Meantime, in his message of 1882, President
Arthur, asserting that "the census returns disclose
an alarming state of illiteracy in certain portions
of the country, where the provision for schools is
grossly inadequate," had urged national aid on a
much broader scale;[37] and in 1883 Senator Blair,
chairman of the Senate Committee on Education,
had introduced a bill providing for the distribution of some $77,000,000 among the states on the
basis of illiteracy. The bill received strong support
from Southern members and passed the Senate
three times. Its final failure was due in part to the
constitutional objection, though in greater measure to other considerations.[38] Not until 1900 did
Congress make an appropriation from the general
funds in aid of education within the states. By an
act passed that year it was provided that whenever the receipts of the sale of public lands should
be insufficient to meet the demands of the act of
1890, the deficit should be met out of "any funds
in the national Treasury not otherwise appropriated."[39] Yet another seven years, and appropriations to supplement the grants which were forth-

coming under the act of 1890 were authorized to the eventual amount of $50,000 per annum for each state and territory.[40]

Then, with the enactment of the Smith-Lever Act of 1914,[41] an entirely new type of federal educational measure sprang into existence. The act in question called for the appropriation of increasing sums, to amount finally to more than four and one-half millions annually, for the promotion of agricultural extension work in the states and territories. The share of each state was determined by its proportion of the rural population of the country and was conditioned on its appropriation each year of an equal sum for the same purpose. Similarly the Smith-Hughes Act of 1917[42] authorized appropriations amounting finally to seven millions per annum, which were to be turned over to the several states in varying proportions for the purpose of coöperating with them in the paying of salaries and the training of teachers of agricultural and industrial subjects and of home economics. Somewhat later the government began rehabilitation work with disabled soldiers, and it is this activity no doubt which suggested the act of 1920, appropriating after 1921 one million dollars annually for coöperating with the states on the now familiar "fifty-fifty" basis, in the vocational rehabilitation of persons disabled in industry;[43] as well as the so-called "Maternity Act" of 1921 "for the promotion of the welfare and hygiene of maternity and infancy."[44] Not only do these measures depend on the literal reading of the "general welfare" clause, they also reveal most strikingly that in its power of expenditure the national government possesses a power of indefinite dimensions to determine state legislative policies and expenditures.[45] The alarmist prophecies of the two Jameses, Madison and Buchanan, have been more than realized—a truly desperate situation, surely, and one against which the Court ought, according to the conventional way of thinking about such things, have long since shattered a lance.

The reassurance to be found in the cases is, nevertheless, meager indeed. That a majority of the Court has been inclined generally to regard Madison's interpretation of the "general welfare" clause as the theoretically correct one, seems not improbable; but that fact only makes more disappointing its persistent refusal to assume the responsibilities of self-government in this field. Both these points are, perhaps, worth a little elaboration.

In the Pacific Railway Cases,[46] in which the scope of the national spending power was first before the Court, that body avoided the question by referring the measures under review to Congress' powers over commerce and the post and to the war power; but in the Gettysburg Electric Railway Case,[47] a few years later, "the great power of taxation to be exercised for the common defense and the general welfare" was invoked in just these words. Nevertheless, when it came to sustain the Federal Farm Loan Banks in 1921,[48] the Court again avoided the major issue, and this in the face of an elaborate brief by Mr. Hughes addressed to the very point.[49]

The latest—and apparently meant to be the last—utterance of the Court is that in the "Maternity Act" Cases, decided June 4, 1923.[50] The act was attacked as tending to defeat the purpose of the Constitution to establish a federal government with limited and enumerated powers; as tending to invade the field of powers reserved to the states by the Tenth Amendment; as in excess of the power granted by Article I, Section 8, Clause 1 of the Constitution; and as requiring from a state which would enjoy the benefits of the act an abdication of its sovereignty.[51] The Court declined to enjoin the Secretary of the Treasury from paying out of the general funds in the Treasury the appropriations necessary to carry the act into effect, either upon the application of a state or on that of an individual taxpayer. As to the former it said: "It cannot be conceded that a state, as *parens patriae*, may institute judicial proceedings to protect citizens of the United States from the operation of the statutes thereof." As regards its relations with its own citizens it is the Federal Government which is *parens patriae* when such representation becomes appropriate.[52] Turning then to the second application, it ruled that the interest of a taxpayer of the United States was not sufficient to support such a suit. "His interest," said the Court, "in the moneys of the Treasury— partly realized from taxation and partly from other sources—is shared with millions of others; is comparatively minute and indeterminable; and the effect upon future taxation, of any payment out of funds so remote, fluctuating and uncertain, that no basis is afforded for an appeal to the preventive powers of a court of equity."[53] The moral seems to be, that so long as Congress has the prudence to lay and collect taxes without specifying the purposes to which the proceeds from any particular tax are to be devoted, it may continue to appropriate the national funds without judicial let or hindrance.

What is more, there are a number of cases in which the Court, contradicting the distinction so insisted upon by Monroe, have in practical effect recognized that national expenditures within the states carry with them certain jurisdictional consequences. Thus property of the national government is not subject to local taxation,[54] while on the other hand Congress may protect it from private molestation.[55] And in the Gettysburg Electric Railway Case,[56] mentioned earlier, the Court was unanimous in sustaining the right of the national government to exercise the power of eminent domain within a state for the laying out of a national park, the expenditure for which was justified in part by reference to the "common defense and general welfare" clause. On the other hand, there is no reason thus far to suppose that the national government may actually compel people to share its bounty contrary to their desires. Suppose, for instance, that Congress should vote money for a school: it could by the cases above alluded to authorize the taking of the necessary land by the power of eminent domain; it could protect both land and buildings from intruders; and neither could be locally taxed. But if attendance at the school were to be required it would have to be by the state, not the national government.

To sum up: Down to 1830 the Hamiltonian or literal—and also liberal—reading of the "general welfare" clause generally governed the application of the national spending power. Between 1830 and the Civil War the Madisonian interpretation of the clause, along the lines of the doctrine of dual federalism, found frequent utterance in Presidential veto messages, but did not in fact prevent national expenditures from spreading over into new, "non-federal," fields. Within the last generation little awareness has been betrayed on the part of either the President or Congress that a constitutional question ever existed with regard to the spending power; and meantime the Court, while showing at times a disinclination to admit the full Hamiltonian thesis, has decisively refused to thrust its sickle into this dread field.

Two general observations are provoked. The first is that, inasmuch as the Supreme Court very inconsiderately refuses to relieve us of the responsibilities of popular government as regards national expenditure, we shall probably have to assume them ourselves if we are to escape national bankruptcy; and this being so, the vital question becomes not that of the relationship of judicial re-

view to governmental expenditure, but that of the
proper relationship of the executive and the legislature in this field of power. While the theory
stated by Monroe and others is that in no other
field is the legislative body more representative
and more immediately responsible, the truth is
that in no other field is it less representative and
less responsible, being constantly exposed when
left to itself to be overridden by corrupt amalga-
mations of thievish interests. For the sorry fact is
that a majority of Congressmen are entirely willing to buy votes so long as they can compound the
felony by doing it with somebody else's money.
Anciently, of course, all proposals for governmental expenditure came from the executive, and the
rôle of the legislative body was merely that of
allowance or disallowance. The Budget Act of
1925 goes a considerable way toward restoring
this wholesome arrangement, but the governing
principle of that act should be made practically
absolute, either by constitutional amendment or by
some further act of heroic self-abnegation by the
Houses. And what makes this reform the more urgent—indeed, imperative—is the extreme im-
probability that the *necessary* expenditures of the
national government will ever return to anything
like their former dimensions.[57]

My second observation is that the success of the
spending power in eluding all constitutional
snares, goes far to envelop the entire institution of
judicial review, as well as its product, constitutional law, in an atmosphere of unreality, even of

futility. With the national government today in possession of the power to expend the social product for any purposes that may seem good to it; the power to make itself the universal and exclusive creditor of private business, with all that this would imply of control; the power to inflate the currency to any extent; the power to go into any business whatsoever, what becomes of judicial review conceived as a system for throwing about the property right a special protection "against the mere power of numbers" and for perpetuating a certain type of industrial organization?

Nor can the reflection be avoided—although, of course, it may be quite mistaken—that if government had been able to regulate private business without having its efforts constantly frustrated by the courts in the name of "due process," the "federal equilibrium," or what not, it might not today be under the compulsion or the temptation to supersede private enterprise directly. In short, having gone in for political democracy, it might have been as well if we had courageously faced the logical consequences of our choice from the outset, instead of trying "to cover our bet" by resigning the ultimate voice as to matters of vital social import to the consciences of nine estimable elderly gentlemen. Today, willy-nilly, we have to face these consequences, and we are ill-equipped in important respects institutionally to do so.

RÉSUMÉ

CONSIDERED for the two fundamental subjects of *the powers of government* and *the liberties of individuals*, interpretation of the Constitution by the Supreme Court falls into three tolerably distinguishable periods. The first, which reaches to the death of Marshall, is the period of the dominance of the *Constitutional Document*. The tradition concerning the original establishment of the Constitution was still fresh and in the person and office of the great Chief Justice the intentions of the framers enjoyed no arid Tithonian immortality. This is not to say that Marshall did not have views of his own to advance; nor is it to say that the historicity of a particular theory concerning the Constitution need be a matter of serious concern save to students of history. It is only to say that the theories which Marshall urged in support of his preferences were, in fact, frequently verifiable as theories of the framers of the Constitution. And one such theory was that the Constitution, to endure, must "be adapted to the various crises of human affairs."

The second period is a lengthy one, stretching from the accession of Chief Justice Taney in 1835 to the death of Justice Brewer in 1910. It is the period *par excellence* of *Constitutional Theory*. More and more the constitutional text fades into the background, and the testimony of the *Federalist*—Marshall's sole book of precedents—ceases to be cited. Among the theories which in one way or other received the Court's sanctifying accolade during this period were the notion of Dual Federalism, the doctrine of the Police Power, the taboo on delegated legislative power, the derived doctrine of Due Process of Law, the conception of liberty as Freedom of Contract, and still others. The sources of these doctrines and the nature of the interests benefited by them have been indicated earlier in these pages, as well as the fact that their net result was to put the national law-making power into a strait-jacket so far as the regulation of business was concerned.

The last period is the present; it is that of *Judicial Review* pure and simple. The Court, as heir to the accumulated doctrines of its predecessors, now finds itself in possession of such a variety of instruments of constitutional exegesis that it is able to achieve almost any result in the field of constitutional interpretation which it considers desirable, and that without flagrant departure from judicial good form. Indeed, it is altogether apparent that the Court was in actual possession and in active exercise of this "sovereign prerogative of choice" some years before most of the Justices were intellectually aware of it, albeit the present Chief Justice was not among the unsophisticates. Even prior to his first appointment to the Supreme Bench, as the successor of Justice Brewer, Mr. Hughes had spoken the notable words quoted at the outset of this volume: *"We are under a Constitution, but the Constitution is what the judges say it is*."[1] Horribly as it must have grated upon the ears of Mr. Hughes's predecessor, this incisive statement describes with accuracy not only an achieved result but a still operative process as well.

So I assert once again, and I do not see how the assertion can be successfully gainsaid, that in approaching the major questions of constitutionality which it will presently be required to pass upon, the Supreme Court is vested with substantially complete freedom of choice whether to sustain or to overturn the New Deal. This freedom, nevertheless, is only of a *particular kind*—it is *jural* freedom, that freedom which the Court has built up for itself piece by piece by its own past practices and precedents in the field of constitutional interpretation. With this freedom there goes inevitably an equally broad *moral* responsibility. The Court —not quite with the active approval of the public, but at least with its acquiescence—had gradually made itself morally answerable for the safety and welfare of the nation to an extent utterly without parallel in judicial annals, past or present. At the same time, while potent to frustrate attempted solutions of the exigent problems which face the government today, it is impotent to provide solutions of its own. And such being the case I venture to suggest that it is the plain duty of the Court to give over attempting to supervise national legislative policies on the basis of a super-constitution which, in the name of the Constitution, repeals and destroys that historic document. (Dual federalism cannot possibly be squared logically with the "su-

premacy" clause; the modern doctrine of due process of law has only the remotest historical justification from the "due process" clause of Amendment
V.) And having done this the Court will be free to
assume again the rôle, so powerfully claimed for it
by Chief Justice Marshall, of pillar and supporter
of the national power and its supremacy.

But certain people have recently raised the cry,
"Back to the Constitution." Just how far back
would they like to go? In view of what has just
been said, the answer seems rather doubtful. Beyond peradventure, the Constitution embodies numerous values which few Americans would wish to
see cast overboard; the question nevertheless remains as to how these can best be conserved.
Burke's words, in his *Reflections*, are very much to
the point: "A state without the means of some
change is without the means of its own conserva-
tion. Without such means it might even risk the
loss of that part of the Constitution which it wished
most religiously to preserve."[2] And it was with a
similar thought in mind that Matthew Arnold
wrote in *Culture and Anarchy:*

We are on our way to what the late Duke of Wellington,
with his strong sagacity, foresaw and admirably described as "a revolution by due course of law." This is
undoubtedly,—if we are still to live and grow, and this
famous nation is not to stagnate and dwindle away on
the one hand, or, on the other, to perish miserably in
mere anarchy and confusion,—what we are on the way
to. Great changes there must be, for a revolution cannot
accomplish itself without great changes; yet order there

must be, for without order a revolution cannot accomplish itself by due course of law. . . . And it [our national right reason] has the testimony of conscience that it is stablishing the State on behalf of whatever great changes are needed, just as much as on behalf of order.[3]

"Back to the Constitution"? Yes; if what is intended is "the Constitution" concerning which the Court has asserted, "It was made for an undefined and expanding future."[4] No; if what is meant is certain doctrines, also sanctioned by the Court at times, which were conceived with the idea in mind of putting the future in cold storage. Fortunately or unfortunately, the future declined to be thus refrigerated. To present-day economic and social conditions the doctrines alluded to have little if any relevance for a community which intends to remain democratic; and if "realities must dominate the judgment," as the Court has said they must,[5] the outlook for such doctrines is not bright. "*Back* to the Constitution"? The first requirement of the Constitution of a progressive society is that it keep pace with that society.

NOTES

INTRODUCTION

1. Maitland once remarked that "accepted commonplaces are powerful agents in moulding a Constitution." *Collected Papers* (Cambridge, 1911), I, 5.

2. The opinion of counsel of the New York Stock Exchange, opposing on constitutional grounds national regulation of that organization, is a good illustration. These gentlemen seem to have become so engrossed with the obstructive possibilities of *Paul* v. *Va.*, 8 Wall. 168 (1868), that they entirely overlooked *West. Un. Tel. Co.* v. *Foster,* 247 U.S. 105, decided fifty years later. Nearly twenty years after the establishment of the Interstate Commerce Commission, a "constitutional lawyer" could argue at length that Congress had no power to regulate interstate railway rates. True, the states could not either, but there were "many political and social evils which our limited and specific Federal system does not alleviate." Edward L. Andrews, "of the New York Bar," New York *Sun,* January 8, 1906.

3. Extract from address at the annual dinner of the American Bar Association, October 22, 1914, 39 *Am. Bar Assoc. Rep.* 114, 119; 7 *Am. Bar Assoc. J.,* 341, 342.

4. See 233 U.S. 389 at 409 (1914).

5. Cf. in this connection Justice Sutherland's opinion in *Funk* v. *U.S.,* 290 U.S. 371, and *Home Building and Loan Assoc.* v. *Blaisdell, ibid.,* 391.

6. *The Movement of Coercion,* reprint of address before New York State Bar Association (January, 1893; 15 pp.), pp. 12–13.

7. *Collected Legal Papers* (New York, 1920), p. 295.

8. See Chief Justice Hughes's opinion in the Blaisdell Case, just referred to; J. Roberts' opinion in *Nebbia* v. *N.Y.,* 291 U.S. 502; J. Brandeis' opinion of dissent in *New State Ice Co.* v. *Liebmann,* 285 U.S. 262, 280–311 (1931), where it is said (p. 311), "To stay experimentation in things social and economic is a grave responsibility"; also Justice Cardozo's luminous exposition in his *Nature of the Judicial Process* (New Haven, 1922), and succeeding volumes, of the types and methods of judicial thinking. Sometimes, too, light is shed by tales told out of school, of which the following may be deemed an example: "It is said that Chief Justice White admitted that

'in my time we relaxed constitutional guarantees from fear of revolution,' and that Chief Justice Taft declared that 'at a conference I announced I had been appointed to reverse a few decisions, and,' with his famous chuckle, 'I looked right at old man Holmes when I said it.' What a pity were these illuminating incidents lost to history save in so far as the court reports will verify them." Judge Bourquin, dissenting, 52 Fed. (2d) 189, at 196 (1931). Mr. Taft's opinion of judges appears to have undergone some change. Defending the Supreme Court at Pocatello, Idaho, in 1911, he said: "I love judges, and I love courts. They are my ideals, that typify on earth what we shall meet hereafter in heaven under a just God." New York *Evening Post,* October 6, 1911. Yet three years later we find him making the startling admission, "Judges are men." *The Anti-Trust Act and the Supreme Court* (New York, 1914), p. 33. "The skepticism of Mr. Justice Holmes and Mr. Justice Brandeis, which recognizes, on the one hand, that doctrines do not govern society, and, on the other, that they can be used wisely and skilfully in governing the Court, is the kind of skepticism which creates great institutions." T. W. Arnold, "The Rôle of Substantive Law and Procedure in the Legal Process," 45 *Harv. L.R.* 617 at 640 (1932).

9. The words are Professor Whitehead's. *Adventures of Ideas* (New York, 1933), p. 44.

CHAPTER I

1. The references are to the Lodge Edition (New York, 1904).

2. The term "people" had in 1787, whether used with reference to the people of the states or of the United States, two quite different meanings. In what may be termed its *Lockian* sense it indicated a population whose members, being possessed of the rights of man, were the ultimate source of all governmental power validly exercisable over them; while in its other, or *Hobbsian* significance, it indicated the supreme authority of an organized political entity. It is evident that Hamilton is here using the term in the former, the Lockian sense; and it appears that this also was the sense which Marshall later gave it. See my *Doctrine of Judicial Review,* 81–108.

3. In *Federalist 28* Hamilton devotes a short paragraph to the same subject, as an offset to his assertion of the right of

the general government to employ military force in the states to enforce its laws. Note also his expectation in *Federalist 16* that the state judges will ordinarily oppose any "conspiracy of the legislature" against the authority of the United States. Lodge Edition, p. 96.

4. 2 *Annals of Congress,* 1891.

5. 2 Dallas 419 (1793).

6. *Ibid.,* p. 457. He also wrote: "To the Constitution of the United States the term *sovereign* is totally unknown. . . . Those who *ordained* and *established* the Constitution . . . might have announced themselves *'sovereign'* people of the United States. But serenely conscious of the *fact,* they avoided the *ostentatious declaration."* It is apparent, however, that Wilson is here using the word "sovereign" in the Lockian, not the Hobbsian sense (cf. n. 2, *supra*), for he straightway adds: "Man, fearfully and wonderfully made, is the workmanship of his all perfect *Creator:* a *State,* useful and valuable as the contrivance is, is the *inferior* contrivance of *man;* and from his *native* dignity derives all its *acquired* importance." 2 Dall. 454–455.

7. *Ibid.,* pp. 470–471.

8. *Hylton* v. *U.S.,* 3 Dall. 171 (1796).

9. 3 Dall. 199 (1796).

10. 130 U.S. 581 (1889); 149 U.S. 698 (1893).

11. See generally Professor Herman V. Ames's invaluable *State Documents on Federal Relations* (Philadelphia, 1906).

12. See my *National Supremacy* (New York, 1913), chap. iii; also n. 2, *supra.*

13. 4 Wheat. 316 (1819). For forerunners of the statement in this case of the doctrine of "adaptative construction," see *Federalist 34*; Marshall's opinion in *Bank of U.S.* v. *Deveaux,* 5 Cr. 61 at 87 (1809); and Story's opinion in *Martin* v. *Hunter's Lessee,* 4 Wheat. 304 at 326 (1816).

14. *Letters and Other Writings* (Philadelphia, 1867), IV, 326, 424–425.

15. J. D. Richardson (ed.), *Messages and Papers of the President* (Washington, 1909), p. 149. Cited hereafter as *Messages and Papers.*

16. *Democracy in America* (New York, 1873), I, 174–175. To some extent De Tocqueville's observations had been anticipated by Montesquieu in more general terms, *Spirit of the Laws,* I, Bk. IX, chap. 1 (Prichard, trans.). See also Polk's tribute, in his Inaugural, to "this most admirable system of well-regulated

self-government among men." *Messages and Papers,* IV, 374–377.

17. Bryce, *The American Commonwealth* (New York, 1891), I, 343.

18. *Writings* (Hunt, ed.), VIII, 447–453; *Letters and Other Writings,* III, 143–147.

19. *View of the Constitution* (Philadelphia, 1837), pp. 3, 100–112.

20. The cases referred to are *Miln* v. *N.Y.,* 11 Pet. 102; *Briscoe* v. *Bank of Ky., ibid.,* 257; and *Charles River Bridge Co.* v. *Warren Bridge, ibid.,* 420.

21. *National Supremacy* (cited *supra,* n. 12), chap. v. The best single source for the constitutional doctrines of the Court under Taney touching the nature of the Union comprises the various opinions of the Justices in the Passenger Cases, 7 How. 283 (1849). The words quoted above regarding the static nature of the Constitution are from the Chief Justice's opinion in *Scott* v. *Sandford,* 19 How. 393 at 426 (1857). For his theory of the balancing rôle of the Court, see his opinions in *Ableman* v. *Booth,* 21 How. 506 at 520–522 (1859) and in *Gordon* v. *U.S.* (published posthumously) 117 U.S. at 700–701. "Dual federalism" is indeed the *leit motif* of the constitutional jurisprudence of the Court for fifty years. In *McElmoyle* v. *Cohen,* 13 Pet. 312 (1839), the "full faith and credit" clause was applied in the light of it. In *United States* v. *Marigold,* 9 How. 560 (1850), the Court on the same basis accepted the principle that a person can be prosecuted for the same act by a state and by the United States—a doctrine it had refused to countenance thirty years earlier. *Houston* v. *Moore,* 5 Wheat. 1, 23 (1820). See also the cases discussed in the text, pp. 12–15. "In strictness there can be no such thing as a conflict between state and nation. The laws of both operate within the same territory, but if in any particular case their provisions are in conflict, one or the other is void." This passage from Cooley's *Principles of Constitutional Law* (3d ed. Boston, 1898) is an excellent statement of the strict doctrine of dual federalism. It is an interesting fact that Cooley, who felt his time to be well spent if he could make two constitutional limitations grow where only one grew before, once tried to project the federal principle into the interior of his own state. In *People* v. *Hurlbut,* 24 Mich. 44 (1871), he held that the right to local self-government rested on a "fundamental law" anterior to the state constitution and hence restrictive

of state legislative power. The doctrine soon spread to other states, and once enjoyed considerable influence, though it seems to be defunct today. See Amasa M. Eaton, "The Right to Local Self-Government," 13 *Harv. L.R.*, 441, 570, 638; 14 *ibid.*, 20, 116 (1900, 1901); also *Trenton* v. *N.J.*, 262 U.S. 182 (1923).

22. 24 How. 66 (1861).

23. 6 Wheat. 264 (1821).

24. 9 *Opinions of Attorney General*, 517.

25. *Messages and Papers*, X, 626.

26. *Ex parte Siebold*, 100 U.S. 371 at 395 (1879).

27. 11 Wall. 113 (1870). In the famous dictum of Chief Justice Chase in *Texas* v. *White*, "the Constitution, in all its provisions, looks to an indestructible Union, composed of indestructible states," the stress is on the indestructibility of the *states* rather than that of the Union. 7 Wall. 700 at 725 (1869).

28. 16 Wall. 36 (1872).

29. 109 U.S. 3 (1883). This was also a period of much writing regarding the nature of the United States as a political entity. J. C. Hurd and O. A. Brownson, in their once famous volumes, elaborated upon Chase's thesis in *Texas* v. *White* (n. 27, *supra*), while Elisha Mulford developed a theory of extreme nationalism along Hegelian lines.

30. 9 Wheat. 1.

31. 6 Wheat. at 413.

32. 9 Wheat. at 189–198.

33. *Brown* v. *Md.*, 12 Wheat. 419 at 439 (1827).

34. 9 Wheat. at 23. While Webster is referring particularly to state power, he evidently regards the doctrine he is stating as being of general application. Pertinent in the same connection is the opinion of Judge Davis of the United States District Court for Massachusetts in the case of the Brigantine *William*, decided in 1808, with reference to Jefferson's Embargo (28 Fed. Cas. 614; No. 16, 700). Answering the argument against the Embargo, that the power to regulate commerce did not embrace the power to prohibit it, Judge Davis said:

"It will be admitted that partial prohibitions are authorized by the expression; and how shall the degree or extent of the prohibition be adjusted but by the discretion of the National Government, to whom the subject appears to have been committed? . . . The power to regulate commerce is not to be confined to the adoption of measures exclusively beneficial to commerce itself, or tending to its advantage; but in our national system, as in all modern sovereignties, it is also to be considered as an instrument for other purposes of general policy and interest. . . . The situation of the United States, in ordinary times, might render legislative interferences relative to commerce less necessary; but the capacity and power of managing and directing it for the advancement of great national purposes seems an important ingredient of sovereignty."

In confirmation of this argument Judge Davis cited the clause of Article I, section 9, of the Constitution interdicting a prohibition of the slave trade till 1808. This clause shows, he asserted, that those who framed the Constitution perceived that "under the power to regulate commerce, Congress would be authorized to abridge it in favor of the great principles of humanity and justice." This case was cited by Chief Justice Hughes as recently as 1933, in support of the proposition that "no one can be said to have a vested right to carry on foreign commerce with the United States." *University of Ill.* v. *U.S.*, 289 U.S. 48 at 57. And see generally my article on "Congress's Power to Prohibit Commerce—a Crucial Constitutional Issue," 18 *Cornell L.Q.*, 477–506 (June, 1933).

35. See especially *McCray* v. *U.S.*, 195 U.S. 27 (1903), and cases there cited.

36. *Letters and Other Writings,* IV, 14–15. Elsewhere, however, Madison lays down the doctrine that "the legitimate meaning of the Instrument must be derived from the text itself." *Ibid.,* III, 228.

37. *Groves* v. *Slaughter,* 15 Pet. 449 (1841).

38. 114 U.S. 622 at 630; 125 U.S. 465 at 482; 141 U.S. 47 at 57; 156 U.S. 577 at 587.

39. 192 U.S. 470 at 492. See also 239 U.S. 326.

40. 175 U.S. 211 at 228. Cf. n. 36, *supra.*

41. *Cooley* v. *Port Wardens,* 12 How. 299.

42. State Freight Tax Case, 15 Wall. 232 (1872); *Robbins* v. *Shelby Taxing District,* 120 U.S. 489 (1887); *Dahnke-Walker Milling Co.* v. *Bondurant,* 257 U.S. 282 (1921).

43. *Bowman* v. *Chic. and N.W. R. Co.,* 125 U.S. 465 (1888); *Leisy* v. *Hardin,* 135 U.S. 100 (1890); *Schollenberger* v. *Pa.,* 171 U.S. 1 (1898); *Austin* v. *Tenn.,* 179 U.S. 343 (1900).

44. *West* v. *Kan. Natural Gas Co.,* 221 U.S. 229 (1911); *Penna.* v. *W. Va.,* 262 U.S. 553 (1923).

45. 221 U.S. at 255. The entire passage is deserving of attention.

46. On the protective aspect of Congress' power, see the cases cited in n. 78, *infra*.

47. *United States* v. *E. C. Knight Co.,* 156 U.S. 1.

48. *Ibid.* at 13.

49. *Ibid.* at 17.

50. 188 U.S. 321 (1903).

51. *Ibid.* at 356–358. The decided inclination of the opinion is, nevertheless, toward the broader view of Congress' power. In addition to the above-cited passages, note J. Harlan's quotation from J. Johnson's opinion in *Gibbons* v. *Ogden:* "The power of a sovereign state over commerce, therefore, amounts to nothing more than a power to limit and restrain it at pleasure." 9 Wheat. at 227. Cf. also n. 34, *supra*.

52. Thus, in an address before the American Bar Association in 1904, Professor H. L. Wilgus of the University of Michigan contended, largely on the basis of the Lottery Case, that the national government could prescribe the conditions upon which manufacturing could be done by companies wishing to engage in interstate commerce. 27 *Am. Bar Assoc. Rep.* 694–753. See also the admirable "Studies in the National Police Power" by R. E. Cushman, reprinted from 3 *Minn. L.R.,* nos. 5, 6 and 7; 4 *ibid.,* nos. 4 and 6 (1919, 1920).

53. Two excellent samples of White's judicial manner at its best—or worst—are his opinions in the Standard Oil Case, 221 U.S. 1, and *Brushaber* v. *Un. Pacif. R.R.,* 240 U.S. 1.

54. 193 U.S. 197 (1934).

55. *Ibid.* at 396–397. "I am happy to know that only a minority of my brethren adopt an interpretation of the law which in my opinion would make eternal the *bellum omnium contra omnes* and disintegrate society so far as it could into individual atoms. If that were its intent I should regard calling such a law a regulation of commerce as a mere pretense. It would be an attempt to reconstruct society. I am not concerned with the wisdom of such an attempt, but I believe that Congress was not entrusted by the Constitution with the power to make it and I am deeply persuaded that it has not tried." J. Holmes, *ibid.* at 411.

56. 207 U.S. 463 (1908).

57. *Ibid.* at 499 and 502–503.

58. *United States* v. *Del. and H. Co.,* 213 U.S. 366.

59. This was the so-called "commodity" clause of the Hepburn Act of 1906.

60. 213 U.S. at 406–408.

61. 247 U.S. 251 (1918). The ensuing discussion of this case is largely taken from my article cited in n. 34, *supra.*

62. 247 U.S. at 278–280. In addition to the cases cited by J. Holmes, see the following cases of later date: *Hamilton* v. *Ky. Distils. Co.,* 251 U.S. 146, 40 Sup. Ct. 106 (1919); *Missouri* v. *Holland,* 252 U.S. 416, 40 Sup. Ct. 382 (1920); *University of Ill.* v. *U.S.,* cited in n. 34, *supra.* In the last-mentioned case the doctrine of constitutional tax-exemption as applied to state property and agencies received a fresh check.

63. See n. 42, *supra.*

64. *Levering and G. Co.* v. *Morrin,* 289 U.S. 103, is interesting in this connection. Here the Court held that petitioners were not entitled under the Anti-Trust Acts to an injunction against defendants forbidding the latter to conspire to halt local building operations in which materials fabricated or bought in other states were used. *"Use* [*sic*] of the materials," said Sutherland, J., "was a purely local matter." *Ibid.* at 107. The Court cited *United Mine Workers* v. *Coronado Coal Co.,* 259 U.S. 344, 410, 411 (1921); *United Leather Workers* v. *Herkert,* 265 U.S. 457 (1923); *Industrial Ass'n* v. *U.S.,* 268 U.S. 64, 77–82 (1925). See also *Loewe* v. *Lawler,* 208 U.S. 274 (1908); *United States* v. *Brims,* 272 U.S. 549 (1926); *Bedford Cut Stone* v. *Journeymen Stone Cutters Assoc.,* 274 U.S. 37 (1927).

65. See *Minn.* v. *Barber,* 136 U.S. 313 (1890); also n. 44, *supra.*

66. The decision in this case, a relic of extreme states' rights days, was substantially overruled in *Henderson* v. *N.Y.,* 92 U.S. 259 (1875).

67. 247 U.S. 275–276.

68. *Ibid.* at 281.

69. See n. 43, *supra.*

70. White, J., in 193 U.S. at 399. See also to the same effect his opinion for the Court in *U.S.* v. *Bennett,* 232 U.S. 299, 305, 306, and the Court's approval of this statement in *Burnet* v. *Brooks,* 288 U.S. 378, 404 (1933). Note also White's sarcastic comment on the argument of the carriers in the Intermountain Rate Cases: "To uphold the proposition it would be necessary to say . . . that the power perished as the result of the act by which it was conferred." Intermountain Rate Cases, 234 U.S. at 493. "The powers [of the United States and states] taken together, ought to be equal to all of the objects of government,

not specially excepted for special reasons, as in the case of duties on exports." *Letters and Other Writings of James Madison,* IV, 250. "If Congress have not the power, it is annihilated for the nation; a policy without example in any other nation, and not within the reason of the solitary one in our own . . . the prohibition of a tax on exports." *Ibid.,* III, 640. See further *ibid.,* pp. 644 and 654; J. Johnson's statement, in *Gibbons* v. *Ogden,* that "the power to regulate commerce here meant to be granted was that power which previously existed in the states." 9 Wheat. 1, 227; Sen. Doc. 29th Cong., 1st Sess., VIII, 410 (1846).

71. 248 U.S. 420 (1919).

72. *Ibid.* at 425.

73. 259 U.S. 20.

74. *Ibid.* at 39.

75. See also citation in n. 60, *supra.* The recent opinion of the Court in the case of *Magnano Co.* v. *Hamilton* (292 U.S. 40), where was sustained a state excise of fifteen cents per pound on all butter substitutes sold within the enacting state, employs language which, by restoring to good standing earlier precedents asserting that "the power to tax is the power to destroy," appears to confine the holding in the Drexel Furniture Co. Case to a maladroitly worded statute.

76. 267 U.S. 432.

77. *Ibid.* at 439.

78. 222 U.S. 20 (1911); 223 U.S. 1 (1912); 234 U.S. 342 (1914); 243 U.S. 332 (1917); 250 U.S. 199 (1919); 257 U.S. 563 (1922).

79. 250 U.S. 203.

80. See n. 47, *supra.*

81. W. H. Taft, *The Anti-Trust Act and the Supreme Court* (New York, 1914), *passim.*

82. 196 U.S. 375. A halfway house to this decision is Addystone Pipe and Steel Co., 175 U.S. 211 (1899), in which the Court largely adopted Mr. Taft's cogent opinion in the Circuit Court of Appeals, 85 Fed. Rep. 271 (1898).

83. 262 U.S. at 35. See also his remarks on the same topic in 258 U.S. at 517–519.

84. 258 U.S. 495 (1922).

85. *Ibid.* at 514–516. See also the Court's opinion in *Lemke* v. *Farmers' Grain Co.,* 258 U.S. 50 at 54 (1922).

86. Act of June 16, 1933, Tit. I, § 1. Those who aver that

Nira is without precedent in our peace-time legislation should examine the Act of September 22, 1922, "to declare a national emergency in the production, transportation, and distribution of coal and other fuel . . . providing for the appointment of a Federal Fuel Distributor . . . and to prevent the sale of fuel at unjust and unreasonably high prices." 42 *Stat. at L.* (67th Cong., 2d Sess.), ch. 413. And nearly a quarter century ago Attorney-General Wickersham, pointing out that "in almost every one of the great staple industries prices have been for years fixed by agreements between the principal producers," asserted that whether or not "a Federal industrial commission should have power to regulate prices," was "a matter for serious consideration." New York *Evening Post,* July 19, 1911.

87. 288 U.S. 344 at 372.

88. 290 U.S. 391 (January 8, 1934).

89. 291 U.S. 502 (March 5, 1934).

90. *Civil Engineering,* III (August, 1933), 421.

91. In Professor Powell's pungent phrase: "The holy name of states' rights is easily forgotten when employers wish their laborers sober and unctuously invoked when they wish their laborers young." *Am. Pol. Sc. R.,* XIX (1925), 305. A word further regarding the connotation of the term *commerce* is appropriate. In this connection writers of conservative tendency sometimes give themselves away in an amusing fashion. Thus in an article written in 1932, under the title "Encroachment by Government on the Domain of Private Business," we encounter the following (my italics): "To invade the *realm of commerce* where the inhabitants carry on their business of agriculture, manufacturing, barter and trade, purchase and sale, transportation and banking, and the numerous complex activities which *make up commerce as a whole,* not only destroys individual initiative and ambition . . .," 18 *Am. Bar Assoc. J.,* 567, 573. In short, in modern conditions, "commerce as a whole" is business as a whole. The organic connection between manufactures and commerce was recognized by Hamilton both in *Federalist No. 35* and in his Report on Manufactures. Specially relevant to the constitutional issue above discussed is his recommendation of an "inspection of manufactured commodities": "This is not among the least important of the means by which the prosperity of manufactures may be promoted. It is, indeed, in many cases one of the most essential. Contributing to prevent frauds upon consumers at home and exporters to foreign

countries, to improve the quality and preserve the character of the national manufactures, it cannot fail to aid the expeditious and advantageous sale of them, and to serve as a guard against successful competition from other quarters." *Works of Alexander Hamilton* (Lodge ed.), IV, 157–158. A federal judge, in ruling recently that the A.A.A. was without power to regulate milk sales entirely within a state, made the distinction between that which "directly" affects interstate commerce and that which affects it in a "secondary" way. *New York Times,* October 20, 1934. The distinction goes back to the Court's opinion in the Sugar Trust Case (see 156 U.S. at 16), where it rests on the assumption that "commerce" is primarily *transportation.* But commerce is primarily *traffic;* and if Congress is entitled to regulate intra-state transportation to make effective its control over interstate transportation, why is it not entitled equally to regulate intra-state sales to make effective its control of interstate sales? Cf. the Shreveport Case, cited in n. 78, *supra.*

92. The Lottery Case (n. 50, *supra*); *Hoke* v. *U.S.,* 227 U.S. 308 (1913), sustaining the "White Slave" Act of 1910, and *Brooks* v. *U.S.* (n. 76, *supra*) mark important stages in the entrance of the national government into the realm of ordinary criminal legislation. The "White Slave" Act was attacked as an invasion of the power of "the states individually to regulate or prohibit prostitution or other immoralities of their citizens." The answer returned by Justice McKenna, speaking for the unanimous Court included the following sage disquisition touching dual federalism: "Our dual form of government has its perplexities, State and Nation having different fields of jurisdiction, . . . but it must be kept in mind that we are one people; and the powers reserved to the states and those conferred on the nation are adapted to be exercised, whether independently or concurrently, to promote the general welfare, material and moral." For recent extensions and proposed extensions of national legislation in the field of ordinary criminal legislation to supplement state laws, see a Washington despatch in the *New York Times* of May 16, 1934, summarizing briefly the six new statutes for "strengthening the hand of the Department of Justice"; and Professor Moley's Report to President Roosevelt on Law Enforcement Measures, *ibid.,* May 24, 1934. Interstate compacts may lessen somewhat the neces-

sity for national legislation of this character, but the usefulness of such devices in modern conditions is rather problematic.

93. *Farmers' L. & T. Co.* v. *Minn.,* 280 U.S. at 211–212 (1930); *Burnet* v. *Brooks,* 288 U.S. at 402 (1933). The circumstance that this statement of fact was made in connection with decisions overturning state legislation should not make it less pertinent to the question of the validity of national legislation.

94. Notwithstanding the practical advantages of the federal system in earlier days, the concept of dual federalism was always highly artificial, owing not a little to the accidental circumstance that the members of the Union were called "states." Being "states," they were by the current lingo of political theory entitled to regard themselves as "sovereign"; and this attribute being conceded them, everything else followed which anybody who chose to argue from such a premise might take it into his head to claim. Again, as has been frequently pointed out by writers, most of our state boundaries are pure projections from the surveyor's compass which even at the outset cut athwart social and economic units arbitrarily, while everything that has happened since has operated to heighten their entire unsuitableness as geographical definitions of governmental units. "Centralization is not an end in itself, either to be advocated or deplored; it is a tendency that has developed as a kind of by-product, in the effort to get the public machinery called government to do the things that the public wants done." W. Brooke Graves, *Uniform State Action, a Possible Substitute for Centralization* (Chapel Hill, 1934), p. 290.

CHAPTER II

1. See my article, "Progress of Constitutional Theory Between the Declaration of Independence and the Meeting of the Philadelphia Convention," *Am. Hist. Rev.,* XXX (April, 1925), pp. 511–536, at 512–513.

2. July 11, 1787; Farrand, *Records,* I, 583.

3. Much of the data will be found in my *Doctrine of Judicial Review;* see especially *ibid.,* pp. 71–75.

4. pp. 488–489 of the Lodge Edition.

5. *Democracy in America* (New York, 1873), I, 304. The entire section, *ibid.,* pp. 297–306, is still worth reading, and along with it chap. vi, on "Judicial Power in the United States."

6. This has seemed to me to be as good a term as any other

to apply to certain of the phenomena which I investigate in my articles entitled "The Doctrine of Due Process of Law Before the Civil War," 24 *Harv. L.R.* 366–385 and 460–479 (1911); and "The Basic Doctrine of American Constitutional Law," 12 *Mich. L.R.* 247–276 (1914).

7. The fundamental character of the property right was frequently asserted in the Philadelphia Convention. Farrand, *Records*, I, 424, 533–534, 541–542; II, 123. Cf. *ibid.*, I, 605. An oft-quoted expression of the "higher law" theory of the source of the right is that of J. Paterson in *Van Horne's Lessee* v. *Dorrance*, 2 Dall. 304 at 310 and 316 (1795). See also Kent, *Commentaries*, II, 319*. "The right of property is before and higher than any constitutional sanction." Ark. Const. of 1874, Art. II, § 22. Thorpe (ed.), *Am. Charters, etc.*, I, 336. Locke's (Second) *Treatise on Civil Government*, chap. v, was perhaps the most important source of the ideas of "the Founding Fathers" regarding property. The property which Locke had in mind, however, did not comprise anything closely analogous to modern investment capital. It embraced only "such outward things as money, lands, houses, furniture and the like." "A Letter Concerning Toleration," *Works* (1727), II, 239 (quoted in Laski, *Grammar of Politics*, p. 181). Pertinent, too, in the same connection is his saying "that the handsome conveniences of life are better than nasty penury." The thought that the security of the property *right* is necessary in order to encourage the production of the *wealth* upon which civilization rests is the thought which is at the basis of Sir Henry Maine's dictum that property and civilization are "inextricably intertwined"; also of Dr. Paul Elmer More's assertion that "to the civilized man *the rights of property are more important than the right to life*" (italics in the original). *Rational Basis of Legal Institutions* (New York, 1923; "Modern Legal Philosophy Series"), p. 311. Returning to "the Founding Fathers," not all of them—at least at all times—accepted the transcendental origin of property. "Property," declared Marshall, in arguing the case of *Ware* v. *Hylton* in 1796, "is a creature of civil society, and subject in all respects to the disposition and control of civil institutions." 3 Dall. at 211. Thirty years later, however, he was of a different opinion. 12 Wheat. at 346. "I think it the better opinion, that the *rights*, as well as the *mode* . . . of acquiring property, and of alienating or transferring, inheriting, or transmitting it is conferred by society; is regulated by *civil* institu-

tions, and is always subject to the rules prescribed *by positive law.*" J. Chase, in *Calder* v. *Bull,* 3 Dall. 386, at 394 (1798). "Private property . . . is a creature of society and is subject to the calls of that society . . . even to its last farthing." Benj. Franklin, "Queries and Remarks, etc.," *Writings* (Smyth, ed.), X, 59. See also his letter of December 25, 1783, to Robert Morris. Yet when the late Vice-President Marshall warned "backward looking men" that the right to inherit and the right to devise "are simply privileges given by the state to its citizens," he was taken vigorously to task by the *New York Times,* which approvingly quoted from a then current opinion of Surrogate R. L. Fowler the statement that "the best thought of the world at the present time is generally conceded to be expressed by the conclusion that the right to dispose of property after death is a natural and inherent right of mankind which cannot be taken away by the state" (*New York Times,* May 14, 1913). "Legislation tending to fix prices . . . is aimed at the correction of the inequalities of wealth which are inevitable under our form of government," and hence is void, held the District of Columbia Court of Appeals in the Minimum Wage Case, and added: "Of the three fundamental principles which underly government . . . the protection of life, liberty, and property, the chief of these is property." 284 Fed. 613 at 617 and 622 (1922). See further W. H. Hamilton, "Property—According to Locke," 41 *Yale L.R.* 864–880 (1932); *Rational Basis of Legal Institutions, supra.*

8. The articles mentioned in n. 6, *supra,* supply confirmatory materials, *passim.*

9. Farrand, *Records,* II, 368, 375, 378, 448, 571, 596, 610, 617, 656; III, 165. "The original meaning of *ex post facto* applies to Civil and Criminal law alike." W. G. Hammond (ed.), *Blackstone's Comms.* I, 132–133, citing English and American cases and other evidence. To same effect is J. Johnson's note, 2 Pet. 681 (1829), criticizing the holding in *Calder* v. *Bull.*

10. Cited in n. 7, *supra.* The reader will discover something of a contradiction between the earlier and the later portions of J. Chase's opinion. In the former he treats the property right as resting on a "higher law" basis; in the latter, as noted above, he treats it as resting on "positive law."

11. 6 Cr. 87. For a fuller criticism of Marshall's opinion, see my *John Marshall and the Constitution* (New Haven, 1919), pp. 147–154. Five years later, in *Terret* v. *Taylor,* 9 Cr. 43 (1815), the Court held simply on general principles that a legis-

lative grant was not revocable, and construed certain acts of Virginia affecting church lands to bring them into conformity with this doctrine.

12. 4 Wheat. 518 (1819); *John Marshall and the Constitution,* pp. 154–172. The *"obligation* of contracts" which Marshall held to be protected by the Constitution was evidently of a transcendental nature. This appears very clearly in his dissenting opinion in *Ogden* v. *Saunders,* 12 Wheat. 213 at 345–350 (1827), where also the notion of "freedom of contract" is adumbrated.

13. 2 Pet. 627.

14. *"Leges et constitutiones futuris certum est dare formam negotiis, non ad facta praeterita revocari, nisi nominatim . . . ,"* Cod. 1, 14, 7. *"Item tempus spectandum erit, cum omnis constitutio futuris formam imponere debeat, et non praeteritis,"* Bracton, b. 4, c. 38, f. 228; Twiss (ed.), III, 530. *Nova constitutio futuris formam imponere debet, non praeteritis,* Coke, 2 *Inst.* 292; Co. Litt., 360a.

15. 7 Johns. 477 at 498 ff.; 1 *Comms.* 455*–456*.

16. On the one hand, all legislation is "prospective," inevitably, in the sense that its enactment must precede its going into effect; on the other hand, most legislation is "retroactive," inevitably, in the sense that it alters somewhat previously existing conditions. The true sense of the term *retroactive* or *retrospective legislation* would appear to be legislation which operates upon past acts as from a time anterior to its passage. The first step to the American conception of retroactive laws as laws which, "though operating only from their passage effect *vested rights* and transactions" (2 Gall. C.C. 105 at 139; 1814) is impossible to trace, but it seems clear that the maxim had been applied in England prior to *Dash* v. *Van Kleeck* in support of statutory constructions favorable to proprietarian interests. See *Couch, qui tam* v. *Jeffries,* 4 Burr. 2460, 2462–2463 (1769); *William* v. *Pritchard,* 4 D. and E. 2 (1790). I have been greatly assisted in the investigation of this topic by an unpublished doctoral thesis of a former student, Dr. Elmer E. Smead, on "Legal Maxims as Instruments of Constitutional Interpretation." H. Goeppert's *Das Princip, "Gesetze haben keine rückewirk. Kraft,"* etc. (1884), is of little value.

17. See n. 15, *supra.*

18. 24 *Harv. L.R.* at 465–466.

19. 12 *Mich. L.R.* at 261–265.

20. Farrand, *Records,* I, 397–401 (Madison's Journal for June 25).

21. *Ibid.,* pp. 421–423 (June 26).

22. Hamilton's words in the Convention were: "An inequality would exist as long as liberty existed, and that it would unavoidably result from that very liberty itself." *Loc. cit.,* p. 424.

23. *Journal of Debates and Proceedings, etc.* (Boston, 1853), pp. 309–313, 317. See also *ibid.,* pp. 247, 254, 276, 278, 280, 284–286, for views of John Adams, Story, *et al.;* also Webster's orations at Plymouth, December 22, 1820, and at the laying of the cornerstone of the Bunker Hill Monument, June 18, 1825, *Writings and Speeches* (National ed. 1903), I, 214 ff., and 259 ff.

24. 12 Wheat. 419 at 443.

25. An excellent sketch of the elaboration of the police power concept, especially by the Supreme Court and in relation to the "commerce" clause, is that of W. J. Hastings, in *Proceedings of the American Philosophical Society,* XXXIX (1900), 359 ff. Hastings points out that legislative interferences with private rights were justified before the rise of the police-power concept by reference to the common-law doctrine of "overruling necessity," *op. cit.,* pp. 414–415. As a matter of fact the police power has never entirely broken away from the tether of the common law. See n. 35, *infra.*

26. 11 Pet. 420.

27. *Ibid.* at 547–548. For the consternation caused by this holding at the time—Kent and Story being foremost among the pessimists—see Charles Warren, *The Supreme Court in United States History* (Boston, 1922), II, 299–306. As a matter of fact, even Marshall's decision in *Providence B'k* v. *Billings,* 4 Pet. 514 (1830), had caused an ominous wagging of heads. See *U.S. Law Intelligencer* (Philadelphia, 1830), II, 383 ff., where it is stated, with evident alarm, "It is indeed openly and daily advanced that no court should be permitted to question the justice and constitutionality of a legislative act."

28. *Satterlee* v. *Matthewson,* 2 Pet. 413 (1829); *Watson* v. *Mercer,* 8 Pet. 110 (1834). In *Loan Association* v. *Topeka,* 20 Wall. 655 (1874), and *Cole* v. *La Grange,* 113 U.S. 1 (1884), we find the Court returning to the earlier practice; the subsequent expansion of judicial review on the basis of the "due process" clause of the Fourteenth Amendment has, however, rendered the practice today unnecessary.

29. 6 How. 507.

30. *Stone* v. *Miss.*, 101 U.S. 814 (1879).

31. "It is settled that neither the 'contract' clause nor the 'due process' clause has the effect of overriding the power of the state to establish all regulations that are reasonably necessary to secure the health, safety, good order, comfort, or general welfare." 232 U.S. 548 at 558. As we shall see later, these words have sometimes to be taken in a rather Pickwickian sense.

32. T. M. Cooley, *Constitutional Limitations,* 487*–495*. It early passed to Iowa, whence it was imported by J. Miller into the Supreme Court. See 20 Wall. 655, 661 and note.

33. The originative tribunals this time were those of Delaware and Pennsylvania. See *Rice* v. *Foster,* 4 Harr. (Del.) 479 (1847); *Parker* v. *Comm.,* 6 Pa. St. 507 (1847); and 24 *Harv. L.R.* 466 n. 91.

34. 12 *Mich. L.R.* 270. The phrase came originally from the Provincial Charter of 1691.

35. *Com.* v. *Alger,* 7 Cush. (Mass.) 53 (1851). In the thirty-sixth year of Elizabeth, Godfrey, counsel for plaintiff in *Edwards* v. *Halinder,* 2 Leon. 93 (1594), contended that the defendant was liable for his acts even though he had not intended to injure plaintiff's property by the use he had made of his own, "for the rule is *sic utere tuo ut alienum non laedas.*" The maxim again appears in Coke's report of Chief Justice Wray's decision in Aldred's Case, 9 Rep. 57 (1611). The maxim was at first confined to cases of injury to real property by adjoining owners, but has since come to be regarded as underlying the whole law of nuisances, and even more broadly. Cf. J. Pitney's use of it in *Hitchman Coal and Coke Co.* v. *Mitchell,* 245 U.S. 229 at 254 (1917).

36. In so doing, however, Shaw only ratified earlier doctrine respecting the police power, especially doctrine which had been developed in New York under the Kentian influence. 12 *Mich. L.R.* 265–269. An extremely interesting application of the maxim in vindication of the police power occurs in the recent case of *Euclid* v. *Ambler Realty Co.,* 272 U.S. 365 (1926), where a zoning ordinance was sustained. Said J. Sutherland: "In solving doubts, the maxim *'sic utere tuo ut alienum non laedas,'* which lies at the foundation of so much of the common law of nuisances, ordinarily will furnish a fairly helpful clew" (*ibid.* at 387). Where this clew was lacking the same Justice

took a much more restricted view of the police power. See n. 90, *infra.*

37. *University of N.C.* v. *Foy,* 2 Hayw. (N.C.) 310 (1804). Cf. Webster's argument in the Dartmouth College Case. 4 Wheat. at 575 and 581–582.

38. *Hoke* v. *Henderson,* 2 Dev. (N.C.) 1 (1833).

39. 24 *Harv. L.R.* 463–466. In addition to the cases there cited see also J. Bronson's words in 3 Hill 469 (1841) and 5 Hill 327 (1843), where the connection between transcendental views of the property right and the derived conception of the "due process of law" appears in clear light. In *Stuart* v. *Palmer,* 74 N.Y. 183 (1878), the "due process" clause is characterized as the most important guaranty of private rights in the state constitution. See further my "Extension of Judicial Review in New York," 15 *Mich. L.R.* 281–313 (February, 1917). Mention should also be made of the recasting during this period of Webster's definition of "law of the land" as "the general law," by the Tennessee Supreme Court. In the case of *Van Zant* v. *Waddell,* 2 Yerg. 260 (1828), this was expanded to "the general law equally binding upon every member of the community . . . under similar circumstances"—in other words, the idea of "equal protection of the laws." J. Catron, who came from Tennessee, based his opinion in the Dred Scott Case on a form of this doctrine, which he referred to the "privileges and immunities" clause of Art. IV, § 2. 19 How. at 526–527.

40. The clause is almost invariably associated in American constitutions, both state and national, with more detailed requirements of a procedural nature, meant for the especial benefit of accused persons; *"noscitur a sociis."* Coke gives the term a purely procedural sense (2 Inst. 50–51). So does Story (*Comms.,* § 1789). The tendency, however, to attach a "higher law" significance to the older and vaguer term "law of the land" (see nn. 37 and 38, *supra*) soon spread to the Supreme Court (*Bank of Columbia* v. *Okely,* 4 Wheat. 235 at 244 [1819]); whereupon the equivalence of this phrase with "due process of law" asserted by Coke (*loc. cit., supra*) worked in the reverse direction, to the aggrandizement of the later clause. We find J. Baldwin writing, in his separate opinion in *Groves* v. *Slaughter,* 15 Pet. 449 (1841): "Being property by the law of any state, the owners [of slaves] are protected from any violations of the rights of property by Congress, under the Fifth Amendment of the Constitution; these rights do not con-

sist merely in ownership, the right of disposing of property of all kinds is incident to it, which Congress cannot touch" (*ibid.* at 515). The opinions in *Hurtado* v. *Calif.,* 110 U.S. 516 (1884), supply further data of historical interest. "Of course, the words 'due process of law' if taken in their literal meaning have no application to this case; and while it is too late to deny that they have been given a more extended signification, still we ought to remember," etc. J. Holmes, dissenting in *Baldwin* v. *Mo.,* 281 U.S. 586, at 595–596 (1930); see also to same effect 274 U.S. at 373, and 285 U.S. at 311.

41. "The larger and better definition of *due process of law* is that it means law in its regular course of administration through courts of justice." 2 Comm. 13*. Cf. 134 U.S. 418 (1890).

42. 12 Wheat. at 444. The maxim has found its most frequent use in the field of taxation. See 181 U.S. 283, 296–302 (1901); 216 U.S. 1, 27 (1910).

43. See especially in this connection the Court's opinions in *Hurtado* v. *Calif.* n. 40, *supra; Mugler* v. *Kan.,* 123 U.S. 623 (1887); and *C.B.Q.R.R. Co.* v. *Chicago,* 166 U.S. 226 (1897). In the earlier New York case of *Perkins* v. *Cottrell,* 15 Barb. 446 (1851), the court invokes in behalf of the property right "the spirit of the constitution which declares" that "no person shall be deprived," etc.; and C.J. Chase uses similar language in his opinion for the Court in *Hepburn* v. *Griswold.* 8 Wall. 603 at 623–624 (1869). It might be answered that "the spirit" of the "due process" clause is not that the property right should enjoy a special status in constitutional law, but that accused persons should have a fair trial.

44. 13 N.Y. 378–488. The opinions, of Comstock, A. S. Johnson, Selden, and Hubbard, in support of the decision, and those of Mitchell and T. A. Johnson in dissent, succeed in anticipating to greater or less extent most of the questions which have arisen subsequently out of the attempt by courts to apply the derived concept of due process of law to the police power.

45. *Ibid.* at 420, 486–487. "The legislature cannot make the mere existence of the rights secured the occasion of depriving a person of any of them." *Ibid.* at 420. "The constitutionality of the law is to be tested the same as though it related to some other and perhaps better species of property. . . . Liquor is not a nuisance *per se,* nor can it be made so by a simple legislative declaration." *Ibid.* at 454. *Contra:* Laws curtailing the

sales of liquors "are valid, not because they impair the value and enjoyment of the property in only a slight degree, which the opponents of this law call a regulation, but because they are not passed with a view to impair the right of property in any degree, but in the exercise of the plain duty of the legislature to prevent pauperism and crime." *Ibid.* at 479–480. "The right of traffic or the transmission of property, as an absolute inalienable right, is one which has never existed since governments were instituted, and never can exist under government." *Ibid.* at 481. There was some initial uncertainty whether the act was voided because it forbade the *sale* of existing stocks of liquor, or because it required their *destruction* in many instances. In 34 N.Y. 657 (1866) the decision is explained as resting on the latter ground. Undoubtedly the most notable reiteration within comparatively recent times of the pure unadulterated Kentian doctrine of vested rights, on the basis of the "due process" clause, was the opinion of Judge Werner, speaking for the Court, in *So. Buf. R. Co.* v. *Ives,* 201 N.Y. 271 (1911), where the first New York workmen's compensation act was disallowed. The defeat of the author of this opinion for reëlection had the result ultimately of rendering the New York Court of Appeals one of the most advanced state courts of final appeal in the Union.

46. 24 *Harv. L.R.* 471–475. The comment of the Rhode Island Supreme Court, which had the Wynehamer decision before it in passing on a similar statute, is especially interesting: "It is obvious that the objection confounds the power of the assembly to create and define an offense with the rights of the accused to trial by jury and due process of law . . . before he can be convicted of it." *Ibid.* at 474. The Wynehamer decision, however, received countenance from the Supreme Court in its decision in the Dred Scott Case a few months later. *Ibid.* at 475–477.

47. 16 Wall. 36 (1872).

48. *Ibid.* at 122. For a sketch of the development of judicial review under the Fourteenth Amendment between 1868 and 1909, see my article, "The Supreme Court and the Fourteenth Amendment," 7 *Mich. L.R.* 643–672 (1909).

49. 94 U.S. 113 (1876).

50. 96 U.S. 97 (1877).

51. *Ibid.* at 103–104.

52. 94 U.S. at 134.

53. The following extract from the late President Hadley's volume on *Economics, an Account of the Relations between Private Property and Public Welfare* (New York, 1896), states the economic credo of *laissez faire* with saving qualifications, as follows:

"In modern politics we have seen that society is better governed by allowing individuals, as far as possible, to govern themselves. In modern economics we have seen that society is made richer by allowing individuals, as far as possible, freedom to get rich in their own ways." *Op. cit.,* 13–14.

But *laissez faire* also derived support from the American belief in inevitable progress, which was in turn aided by the rapid spread during this period of the doctrine of evolution. In "evolution" there was a force, people thought, which was bound to produce the millennium sooner or later, though just how it could be stopped working once the millennium was produced, nobody pointed out. For some severe words on the "demoralizing ethic" resulting from the belief that "progress is inevitable anyhow," see John Dewey, *Character and Events* (New York, 1929), II, 824. See further n. 70, *infra.*

54. 109 U.S. 3 (1883).

55. Cited in n. 40, *supra.*

56. 110 U.S. at 535–536. For an early employment of the term "constitutional limitations," see E. P. Hulbert, *Essays on Human Rights and Their Political Guaranties* (New York, 1845), chaps. iv and v.

57. *Butchers' Union Co.* v. *Crescent City Co.,* 111 U.S. 746 at 765. See also his dissent in *Campbell* v. *Holt,* 115 U.S. 620 at 630.

58. *In re Jacobs,* 98 N.Y. 98 (1885); *People* v. *Marx,* 99 N.Y. 377 (1885); and *State* v. *Goodwill,* 33 W. Va. 179 (1889), are illustrations. See also n. 69, *infra.*

59. Dr. B. B. Kendrick deserves the credit for tracking down the Journal and restoring it to the world. See his *Journal of the Joint Committee of Fifteen on Reconstruction* ("Columbia Studies in Hist., Econs., and Pub. Law," 1914). A report of Conkling's argument, which was delivered in December, 1882, is to be found in *United Supreme Court Records and Briefs,* for 116 U.S. The case here involved was *San Mateo Cy.* v. *So. Pac. R.R. Co.,* 116 U.S. 138, which was dismissed as having become moot. The same point was again at issue in *Santa Clara Cy.* v. *So. Pac. R.R. Co.,* 118 U.S. 394. At the outset of the case the Chief Justice announced that the Court did not wish to hear

argument on the question whether the word "person" in the "equal protection" clause of the Fourteenth Amendment applied "to these corporations. We are of opinion that it does." The company lost the case on a subordinate point.

60. 116 U.S. 307 at 331.

61. 118 U.S. 356 (1886).

62. Cited in n. 43, *supra.*

63. 123 U.S. 660–661 (1886).

64. 127 U.S. 678.

65. *Ibid.* at 685. I have italicized the words quoted because they indicate that at that date the Court regarded the important question to be that of the scope of judicial power in determining facts, rather than whether the facts were to be used in behalf of or against the statute under review.

66. C. W. Collins, *The Fourteenth Amendment and the States* (Boston, 1912), pp. 188–206.

67. See C. E. Shattuck, "The True Meaning of the Term 'Liberty' in Those Clauses in the Federal and State Constitutions Which Protect 'Life, Liberty, and Property,'" 4 *Harv. L.R.* 365–392 (1891). For a unique anticipation of the modern concept of "liberty," dating from before the Civil War, see *Ex parte Newman,* 9 Calif. 502 (1858), where a Sunday observance law was set aside as conflicting with "freedom of worship" and "inalienable rights" protected by the state constitution. Curiously enough, in view of his later attitude, Judge Stephen J. Field dissented, and his dissent later became the doctrine of the court. 18 Calif. 685.

68. See n. 53, *supra.*

69. J. B. Thayer, *Cases on Constitutional Law,* I, 918–944, contains several of the leading cases showing the struggle. Especially instructive is the case of *State* v. *Loomis,* 115 Mo. 307 (1893), where both sides of the question are presented. Thayer himself opposed the new concept of "liberty," while Tiedeman, editor of the *Am. L.Reg.,* strongly supported it. See also Dean Pound's excellent discussion of these and other like cases in his "Liberty of Contract in American Constitutional Theory," *Rational Basis of Legal Institutions* (cited n. 7, *supra*), chap. xi.

70. See his dissent in *Budd* v. *N.Y.:* "The paternal theory of government is to me odious. The utmost possible liberty to the individual, and the fullest possible protection to him and his property, is both the limitation and duty of government." 143

U.S. at 551 (1892). To the same general effect is his much earlier dissent in *St.* v. *Nemaha Cy.,* 7 Kan. 549, 555–556 (1871). The Budd Case, while before the New York Court of Appeals, also elicited some strongly *laissez faire* views from Judge (later Justice) Peckham. The law there involved, fixing the charges of elevators, was, he asserted, a harking back to principles of the seventeenth and eighteenth centuries, and ignored "the more correct ideas which an increase of civilization and a fuller knowledge of the fundamental laws of political economy and a truer conception of the proper functions of government have given us today." Such legislation was "vicious in its nature and communistic in its tendencies." 117 N.Y. 1 at 47 (1889). Judge Gray was of a similar opinion: "By reason of the changed conditions of society and a truer appreciation of the functions of government, many things have fallen out of the range of the police power, as formerly recognized, the regulation of which would now be regarded as invading personal liberty." *Ibid.,* 21–22. It was, of course, Peckham's opinion in the Lochner Case, 198 U.S. 45 (1905), that evoked from J. Holmes his famous protest that "the Fourteenth Amendment does not enact Mr. Herbert Spencer's social statics." *Ibid.* at 75. See also A. T. Mason's *Brandeis: Lawyer and Judge in the Modern State* (Princeton Univ., 1933), chap. v, and Max Lerner, "The Supreme Court and American Capitalism," 42 *Yale L.J.* 668–701 (1933).

71. The grand objection to the doctrine of "freedom of contract" as it has been frequently enforced by the courts in labor cases is conveyed in the striking statement of the Lord Chancellor in *Vernon* v. *Bethell,* 2 Eden 113: "Necessitous men are not, truly speaking, free men." Quoted by J. Curtis in *Russell* v. *Southard,* 12 How. 139 at 152 (1851). The Supreme Court has more than once taken account of labor's disadvantage in bargaining power in passing on legislation under Amendment XIV, though at other times it has refused to admit the force of this consideration. See 169 U.S. 366 at 397, and 183 U.S. 13 at 21. Compare 236 U.S. 1. See also 259 U.S. 530.

72. Chas. Warren, "The New 'Liberty' under the Fourteenth Amendment," 39 *Harv. L.R.* 431–465 (1926).

73. 9 Wheat. 738.

74. *Ibid.* at 748.

75. *Gov. of Ga.* v. *Madrazo,* 1 Pet. 110 (1828).

76. The cases are sufficiently reviewed in *In re Ayers,* 123

U.S. 443 (1887), and *Pennoyer* v. *McConnaughy,* 140 U.S. 1 (1891).

77. The above note.

78. *In re Debs,* 158 U.S. 564.

79. The elbowing process began in the Pennoyer Case, n. 76, *supra;* the basis for plenary judicial review of rates set by state authority was laid in *Chicago M. & St. P. Ry.* v. *Minn.,* 134 U.S. 418 (1890).

80. 169 U.S. 466. *Ex parte Young,* 209 U.S. 123 (1908) adds nothing to the earlier holding. Interest in the case was due to political causes, which resulted in Congressional legislation creating the so-called "statutory court" of three judges to handle rate cases. U.S.C. Tit. 28, § 380. The recent "Johnson amendment" to this section undertakes to abolish altogether this jurisdiction of the Federal courts (which did not exist prior to 1875), thereby forcing the utilities to have recourse first to the state courts, from whose decision an appeal then lies on writ of error to the Supreme Court. On the constitutional question thus raised see the next chapter, n. 102.

81. April 30, last, the Court finally disposed of a case involving the validity of telephone rates which were set by the Illinois Commission in 1923, and which were immediately enjoined by a federal court. *Lindheimer* v. *Ill. Bell Tel. Co.,* 292 U.S. 151. It ought to be noted that when an officer is sued for damages for an allegedly illegal act, he alone is affected by the suit, whatever its outcome. But when an officer is enjoined from doing an allegedly unconstitutional act prior to a final determination of the issue, the *government itself* has been enjoined if it turns out finally that the constitutional objection to the officer's proposed act was baseless. This consideration applies equally, of course, in the case of state officers claiming the protection of the Eleventh Amendment and in that of officers of the national government, which on general principles may not be sued without its consent.

82. For a more detailed account of this development see the survey in *Willoughby on the Constitution* (2d ed., 1929), II, 820–841. The concept of "business affected with a public interest" is subjected to damaging criticism in two excellent articles by W. H. Hamilton, in 39 *Yale L.R.* at 1089 (1930), and B. P. McAllister, in 43 *Harv. L.R.* at 759 (1930). In *Nebbia* v. *N.Y.,* 291 U.S. 502, the Court appears to reject it—certainly it greatly reduces its significance.

83. *Home Tel. and Tel. Co.* v. *Los Angeles,* 227 U.S. 278 (1913); cf. *Ex parte Virginia,* 100 U.S. 339 (1879).

84. See 209 U.S. at 150.

85. The doctrine of *Smyth* v. *Ames* concerning the availability of injunction proceedings against allegedly unconstitutional state acts did not long remain confined to rate cases, or to the Fourteenth Amendment. See, e.g., the following cases: *Truax* v. *Raich,* 239 U.S. 33 (1915); *Adams* v. *Tanner,* 244 U.S. 590 (1916); *Looney* v. *Crane Co.,* 245 U.S. 180 (1917); *Bowman* v. *Continental Oil Co.,* 256 U.S. 642 (1921); *Weaver* v. *Palmer Bros., Co.,* 270 U.S. 402 (1926). In all these cases the lower courts' injunctions were sustained. For instances of such injunctions being reversed, see the Minnesota and Missouri Rate Cases, 230 U.S. 352 and 474 (1913).

86. J. B. Thayer's "Origin and Scope of the American Doctrine of Constitutional Law," 7 *Harv. L.R.* 129 (1893), furnishes ample evidence on this point.

87. 169 U.S. 366.

88. 198 U.S. 45.

89. *Ibid.* at 56 and 61.

90. *Adkins* v. *Children's Hospital,* 261 U.S. 525.

91. *Ibid.* at 546; approved by the entire Court in *Wolff Packing Co.* v. *Industrial Ct.,* 262 U.S. 522 at 534 (1923).

92. See, for instance, the opinions of JJ. Holmes and Hughes in 219 U.S. at pp. 104 and 549, respectively. This approach has generally characterized the Court's application of the "equal protection" clause. See 194 U.S. 267, and 232 U.S. 138; cf., however, 165 U.S. 150, and 257 U.S. 312.

93. 208 U.S. 412.

94. On "the Brandeis brief" and its lineal descendant, "the Brandeis opinion," see the excellent chapters in A. T. Mason's *Brandeis: Lawyer and Judge in the Modern State,* pp. 102–178.

95. See, e.g., 244 U.S. 590; also citation in n. 90, *supra.*

96. The previous note; also *New State Ice Co.* v. *Liebmann,* 285 U.S. 262 at 280–311 (1932); and *Liggett and Co.* v. *Lee,* 288 U.S. 517 at 541–586.

97. 264 U.S. 504. *Weaver* v. *Palmer Bros.,* 270 U.S. 402 (1926) is a similar performance. Cf. *Petersen Baking Co.* v. *Bryan,* 290 U.S. 570.

98. 264 U.S. at 534.

99. *Ibid.*

100. 281 U.S. at 595 (1930).

101. Mr. Herbert Croly said something to this effect in his *Promise of American Life*.

102. 19 How. at 454–455.

103. *Hepburn* v. *Griswold*, 8 Wall. 603 (1870), overruled in *Knox* v. *Lee*, 12 Wall. 457 (1871). On this once famous chapter in the Court's history see Charles Warren, *The Supreme Court in United States History* (Boston, 1922), III, chap. 31; and Louis B. Boudin, *Government by Judiciary* (New York, 1932), I, 20–28; II, chap. 25.

104. *Pollock* v. *Farmers' L. & T. Co.*, 157 U.S. 429, and 158 U.S. 601 (1895). The case was originally a moot case, and the lower court's taking jurisdiction of it was in substantial defiance of § 3224 R.S.

105. 157 U.S. at 534 and 544.

106. 3 Dall. at 177.

107. 157 U.S. at 607. J. Field held that the exemption in the act violated the "uniformity" clause of Art. 1, § 8, p. 1; and I have come to the conclusion that this view was shared by three others of the majority in 157 U.S. Mr. Allan Nevins seeks to show in an appendix to his recent *Life of Cleveland* that the Justice who changed his mind on the second argument of the case was Justice Brewer, but a better case can be made for Gray. Brewer was quite as conservative as his uncle, Field, quite as fearful of socialism, and I know of no case, unless this be one, in which they parted company. Gray, on the other hand, was one of the Court which in *Springer* v. *U.S.*, 102 U.S. 586 (1880), sustained a Federal income tax as not "direct." So the only question in regard to him is just *when* he changed his mind—whether that occurred *before* or *after* the first argument in the Pollock Case.

108. *Eisner* v. *Macomber*, 252 U.S. 189 (1920).

109. The cases are lined up in Justice Stone's opinion for the Court in *Bromley* v. *McCaughn*, 280 U.S. 124 (1929), where a divided Court sustained the Federal Gift Tax as an excise.

110. See my "Constitutional Tax Exemption" in Supplement to the *National Municipal Rev.*, XIII, No. 1 (January, 1924), at pp. 58–59.

111. *Standard Nut Margarine Co.* v. *Miller*, 284 U.S. 498 (1932).

112. *Heiner* v. *Donnan*, 285 U.S. 312, especially at 326 (1932). Cf. 240 U.S. 1 at 24–25. The invocation of the Fifth Amend-

ment in the Adair Case, 208 U.S. 161 (1908) might be ignored as *obiter,* the measure involved having been already pronounced void as not a regulation of commerce. Nor is the Adkins Case relevant to the issue, since Congress was there legislating for the District of Columbia.

113. See my *Doctrine of Judicial Review,* 144–154.

114. *Supra,* pp. 68–71 and accompanying notes.

115. J. Holmes has spoken on this point a number of times. See Alfred Lief (ed.), *Dissenting Opinions of Justice Holmes,* pp. 282, 290, 297, 299 for citations. "I am the last man in the world to quarrel with a distinction simply because it is one of degree. Most distinctions, in my opinion, are of that sort, and are none the worse for it." J. Holmes in 201 U.S. 562 at 631. For a different view see C.J. Marshall in 4 Wheat. 316 at 423, and 12 Wheat. 419 at 439.

116. See 127 U.S. 678; 208 U.S. 412; 211 U.S. 31.

117. I have seen it reliably stated that stocks of companies listed on the "Big Exchange" whose total value at one time in 1929 was $89,000,000,000 had by a certain date in 1932 shrunk to $14,000,000,000. "The ups and downs of business confiscate more property in one month than our legislatures and administrative commissions in a decade." W. H. Hamilton in article cited in n. 7, *supra.*

118. *Human Nature and Conduct* (New York, 1930), pp. 144–145.

119. See *Rational Basis of Legal Institution, passim,* n. 7, *supra.*

120. "Democracy has no more persistent nor insidious foe than the money power to which it may say, as Dante said when he reached in his journey through hell the dwelling of the God of Riches, 'Here we found wealth, the great enemy.' The enemy is formidable because he works secretly, by persuasion or deceit rather than by force and so takes men unawares." James (Viscount) Bryce, *Modern Democracies* (New York, 1921), II, 486.

121. *Nebbia* v. *N.Y.,* n. 82, *supra.*

122. J. Holmes had earlier ventured the suggestion that "the notion that a business is clothed with a public interest and has been devoted to a public use is little more than a fiction intended to beautify what is disagreeable to the sufferers." 273 U.S. 418 at 446 (1927). The opinion (dissenting) applies the

acid solvent of common sense to several *clichés* of current constitutional law.

123. J. Holmes, 244 U.S. 205 at 222.

CHAPTER III

1. London ed. of 1747, pp. 37, 45, 49, 240, 257, 363, 369. And see generally my articles entitled "The 'Higher Law' Background of American Constitutional Law," 42 *Harv. L.R.* 149–185, 365–409 (December, 1928; January, 1929).

2. Welldon trans. (1905), Bk. III, 15–16.

3. *Op. cit.*, p. 4.

4. Holland, *Elements of Jurisprudence* (13th ed., 1924), p. 44 n.

5. See 42 *Harv. L.R.* (cited in n. 1, *supra*) at 149–157, and numerous further references there given.

6. *Ibid.* at 164–169; C. H. McIlwain, *The Growth of Political Thought in the West* (New York, 1932), chaps. v and vi, *passim*. However, thinkers of the later Middle Ages had begun to take account of a lawmaking power and of the necessity therefor in order to meet emergencies and changing circumstances. *Ibid.* at 217–218, 221, 244, 256, 286. For modern revivals of the notion of legislation as an act of discovery, see Hugo Krabbe, *The Modern Idea of the State* (Sabine and Shepard, tr. New York, 1922), and the writings of the late Leon Duguit. The latter taught that, in order to be *droit* and hence binding, *loi* (legislative law) must further "social solidarity." No *loi* was binding simply as an expression of the will of the lawmaker, as no human being has any capacity to impose his will on his fellows—an idea which may have been derived from the writings of certain Papalists. McIlwain, *op. cit.*, p. 51.

7. Chap. xxvi, "Of Civil Laws" (Morley ed.), pp. 123–124. The Hobbsian conception of law has been well phrased thus: "It is merely the exercise of power, and the end to which the power is directed is not relevant to its authority as a command." C. K. Allen, *Law in the Making* (Oxford, 1927), p. 239.

8. "With regard to such points as are not indifferent, human laws are only declaratory of, and act in subordination to the former," i.e., "the law of nature and the law of revelation." 1 *Comms,* Introd., p. 43. "No human laws are of any validity, if contrary to this [law of nature]." *Ibid.,* p. 41. "But if the Par-

liament will positively enact a thing to be done which is unreasonable, I know of no power that can control it; . . . for that were to set the judicial power over that of the legislature, which would be subversive of all government." *Ibid.,* p. 91. "It [Parliament] can, in short, do everything that is not naturally impossible; and therefore some have not scrupled to call its power, by a figure rather too bold, the omnipotence of Parliament." *Ibid.,* chap. ii, p. 162.

9. Published in 1776, when Bentham was twenty-eight. The great significance of the work is its dismissal of the idea that loyalty to past institutions is a *duty* of the legislator. The issue is thus drawn between Humanitarianism and the older systems of ethics, and the way paved for a system of legislation simply on the doctrine of "the greatest good to the greatest number."

10. Quoted by A. C. McLaughlin, in *The Courts, the Constitution, and Parties* (Chicago, 1912), pp. 69–70. For the contrasted phrases *"jus dicere"* and *"jus dare,"* see Bacon, *Essays,* "Judicature."

11. See J. W. N. Sullivan, *The Limitations of Science* (New York, 1933), pp. 104–108.

12. While owing much to Newton's great discoveries and to deism, the confusion of moral and physical "natural laws" is not modern. For a learned treatment of the subject see John Dickinson's *Adminstrative Justice and the Supremacy of Law* (Harvard Univ., 1927), pp. 110–118, especially nn. 7 and 15.

13. *New York Times,* February 28, 1934.

14. Closely paralleling Mr. Davis' screed is the following quotation from an address, in 1921, by Mr. Justice Sutherland, then United States Senator from Utah: "There is nothing more unfortunate in governmental administration than a policy of playing fast and loose with great economic and political principles which have withstood the strain of changing circumstance and the stress of time and have become part of our fundamental wisdom. . . . Conditions which such a principle governs may change—indeed, in this forward moving world of ours, they must change—but the principle itself is immutable; once righteous, it is always righteous. . . . There are certain fundamental social and economic laws which are beyond the power, and certain underlying governmental principles, which are beyond the right of official control, and any attempt to interfere with their operation inevitably ends in confusion, if not disaster." 44 *Reports N.Y. St. Bar Assoc.,* 263 ff. (quoted in

Brooklyn L.R., April, 1934, p. 317 n.). Accurately speaking, of course, a "natural law" in the scientific sense cannot be *over-ridden*—otherwise, it was not a *law* to begin with. Furthermore, so far as "economic laws" are concerned, it is apparent that a deliberate "violator" thereof may profit immensely, as when the monopolist "violates" the "law of supply and demand." Such "violations," however, do not particularly interest Justice Sutherland and Mr. Davis. What they reprehend is *governmental* "violations" of these alleged laws. In other words, they value these laws particularly as *restraints on government.*

15. The rôle of legislation in the early history of the law has unquestionably been vastly underestimated by modern writers. The influence of Savigny and Maine tended all in this direction. Savigny exalted custom. For an interesting adaptation of his attitude to criticism of the Sherman Anti-Trust Act, see J. C. Carter's *Law, Its Origin, Growth and Function* (New York, 1907). Maine's *Ancient Law,* if not definitely influenced by *laissez faire* ideas, certainly lent these ideas important support among the legal profession. On the general subject of the relation of custom and legislation and of judicial and legislative power, see the excellent work by Allen, cited in n. 7, *supra,* especially chap. vi and pp. 349–356.

16. *Inst.,* I, 2.

17. *De Republica Anglorum* (Alston, ed. Cambridge, 1906), Bk. II, chap i.

18. For a sweeping dismissal of the idea of extra-constitutional limitations on legislative power, see J. Comstock's opinion in the Wynehamer Case, 13 N.Y. 378 at 390–392. To the same effect is Cooley's *Constitutional Limitations,* 164* ff. In point of fact the Court has within recent decades listened to and taken account of arguments based on the theory that there are extra-constitutional restrictions upon legislative power which are judicially enforcible. See Justice Day for the Court in *Dorr* v. *U.S.,* 195 U.S. 138 (1904); and J. McKenna for the Court in *Gilbert* v. *Minn,* 254 U.S. 325, at 332 (1920). But in the main the statement in the text is accurate.

19. 42 *Harv. L.R.* at 157.

20. J. W. Allen, *op. cit.* (New York, 1928), p. 20; see also *ibid.,* pp. 24, 70, 71.

21. See my "Moratorium over Minnesota," 82 *U. of Pa. L.R.* 311 at 314–315. "No one swears to support it [the Constitution] as he understands it; but to support it simply as it is in truth."

So spoke Henry Clay in his speech on the Veto Power, July 12, 1832. Benton, *Abridg.,* XI, 537.

22. The position of such critics is closely comparable with that represented by Calhoun's doctrine of nullification. This asserted the right of any state in the Union to nullify any act of Congress on constitutional grounds until and unless three fourths of all the states agreed to an amendment to the Constitution specifically conferring the challenged power. In other words, the critics assume the chief point to be proved, viz., that a constitutional amendment is necessary.

23. On this point see the suggestive article by Mr. Louis B. Boudin, "The Anarchic Element in the Notion of a Higher Law," 8 *N.Y.U.L.Q.R.* 1–40.

24. 42 *Harv. L.R.* at 180–183.

25. *Ibid.* at 367–380, and notes.

26. *Federalist 78,* p. 485 (Lodge ed.).

27. Interesting in this connection is the article of Herbert Pope, entitled "The Fundamental Law and the Power of the Courts," 27 *Harv. L.R.* 45–67 (1913).

28. *Luther* v. *Borden,* 7 How. 1. (1849).

29. The Myers Case, 272 U.S. 52 (1926), is a clear illustration; cf. *Ex parte Hennen,* 13 Pet. 230 (1838).

30. See my *Doctrine of Judicial Review,* pp. 21–23 and 66–68, and references there compiled.

31. 10 *Stat. at L.* 604, c. 71, § 1.

32. 15 *Stat. at L.* 223, c. 249, § 1.

33. 38 *Stat. at L.* 731, c. 323, § 6 (1914).

34. 47 *Stat. at L.* 70, c. 90 (1932).

35. On the other hand, in enacting section 7a of Nira, stipulating for labor the right to bargain collectively, Congress must have been greatly encouraged by the attitude shown by the Court in *Tex. and N.O. R.R. Co.* v. *Brotherhood,* 281 U.S. 548 (1930).

36. 42 *Harv. L.R.* 161.

37. Cod. I, 14, 12. See also *ibid.,* I, 17, 2, 21.

38. Pound and Plucknett, *Readings on the History and System of the Common Law* (Rochester, 1927), pp. 117–118 (Langbridge's Case, 1345; Y.B. 18–19 Edward III).

39. Quoted in J. C. Gray, *The Nature and Sources of the Law* (New York, 1909), § 229.

40. I am thinking, of course, most especially of Jerome Frank's *Law and the Modern Mind* (New York, 1930). For a

critical survey of Frank's and kindred theories, see "Some American Interpretations of Law" by A. L. Goodhart, in *Modern Legal Theories* (Oxford, 1933), pp. 1–20. The "realist school" seems to have got its cue from Justice Holmes's famous definition of law as "prophecies of what the courts will do in fact" (*Collected Legal Papers*, p. 173). The definition leaves open the vital question of what data are to be considered in venturing such a prophecy; and in this ample space Mr. Frank and his followers disport themselves considerably. Also they build upon Professor Gray's contention (*op. cit.* in previous note) that a legislature is inherently unable to make laws in such terms as not to leave the real law-making power with the courts in applying them. The underlying idea seems to be that the same thing cannot be said twice. But if this is so, then it follows that courts, too, are unable to state effective *rules*. It follows that there is *no law,* only decisions; that courts do not *say* anything of importance, but only *do* things. And Mr. Frank and others draw this conclusion.

41. As Justice Holmes remarks, "You can give any conclusion a logical form." *Collected Legal Papers* (New York, 1920), p. 181.

42. 9 Wheat. at 866 (1824).

43. Cf., e.g., *Leisy* v. *Hardin,* 135 U.S. 100, with *Plumley* v. *Mass.,* 155 U.S. 461; also with *Brown* v. *Houston,* 114 U.S. 622.

44. 19 How. at 426. "A constitution is not to be made to mean one thing at one time, and another at some subsequent time, when the circumstances may have so changed as perhaps to make a different rule in the case seem desirable." So says Cooley in his *Constitutional Limitations.* "No instrument can be the same in meaning today and forever and in all men's minds. As the people change, so does their written constitution change also." So speaks Cooley the historian of Michigan. Judge C. F. Amidon, "The Nation and the Constitution," address before the American Bar Association, 1907 (Reprint), pp. 3–4.

45. See pp. 68–71, *supra.*

46. 12 How. 443 (1851). The case overturned was that of the *Thomas Jefferson,* 10 Wheat. 428.

47. The objections to invoking the supposed "intention" of the legislator are excellently stated in Carron de Malberg's *Théorie Générale de l'État* (Paris, 1920), I, § 237, where other writers are cited. See also Justice Sutherland's opinion in *Rus-*

sel Motor Car Co. v. *U.S.* 261 U.S. 514 (1923), for citation of cases forbidding resort by a court to legislative debates for extrinsic aid in interpreting a statute; and 47 *Harv. L.R.* 1266–1268 (1934) for the alternative view.

48. See the list of overruled cases in constitutional law in J. Brandeis' dissenting opinion in *Burnet* v. *Coronado Oil and Gas Co.,* 285 U.S. 393 at 407–410, nn. 2 and 4 (1932). Since then several other similar cases have occurred, including "the New York Milk Case" (*Nebbia* v. *N.Y.*). "In matters involving the meaning and integrity of the Constitution, I can never consent that the text of that instrument shall be overlaid and smothered by the glosses of essay-writers, lecturers, and commentators. Nor will I abide the decisions of judges, believed by me to be invasions of the great *lex legum.* I, too, have sworn to observe and maintain the Constitution. I possess no sovereign prerogative by which I can put my conscience into commission. I must interpret exclusively as that conscience shall dictate." J. Daniel, 5 How. 540 at 612 (1847). See also Bancroft, *History* (Author's last revision), VI, 350; and G. T. Curtis, *Constitutional History of the United States* (New York, 1897), I, 69–70. A fresh review of the subject from a somewhat novel angle is given by M. P. Sharp, "Movement in Supreme Court Adjudication—a Study of Modified and Overruled Decisions," 46 *Harv. L.R.* 361–403, 593–637, 795–811 (1933). "Now that we recognize that the constitutional provision against impairing the obligation of contracts applies only to legislative action, there seems to be no good reason for recognizing the doctrine of *stare decisis* at all. The courts, like the legislatures, should never alter the law oftener than seems necessary for the good of society, but the need of change being granted, the existence of a wrong decision should not be allowed to block the way of reform." Henry Upson Sims, Presidential Address, American Bar Association, Chicago, August 22, 1930. 53 *Am. Bar Assoc. Rep.* 199.

49. *Cong. Record,* March 24, 1934, p. 5480. Justice Story and Chancellor Kent gave vent to similar lamentations following the accession of Taney. See chap. ii, n. 27, *supra.*

50. Consider, e.g., the various holdings in 257, 262, and 268 U.S. Reports, bearing on the subject of "open combinations" under the Anti-Trust Acts. The maxim that substance and not form should control has aided the Court at times to emphasize such elements of a case as it chose to. See, e.g., *Ex parte*

Young, 209 U.S. 123. Chief Judge Pound remarks dryly: "No two cases are exactly alike. A young attorney found two opinions in the New York Reports where the facts seemed identical although the law was in conflict, but an older and more experienced attorney pointed out to him that the names of the parties were different." *N.Y. Bar Assoc. Bul.,* June, 1933, p. 267.

51. It should not, however, be supposed that the *judicial dilemma,* if one may so term it, is peculiar to American constitutional law. Consider, for instance, the argument by Sjt. Morgan in *Colthirst* v. *Bejushin* (4 Edw. VI; 1551): "Further, there are two principal things from whence arguments may be drawn, that is to say, our maxims, and reason, which is the mother of all laws. But maxims are the foundations of the law, and the conclusions of reason, and therefore they ought not to be impugned, but always to be admitted; yet these maxims may by the help of reason, be compared together, and set one against another (although they do not vary), where it may be distinguished by reason that a thing is nearer to one maxim than to another, or placed between two maxims, nevertheless they ought never to be impeached or impugned, but always be observed and held as firm principles and authorities of themselves." Plowden, *Comms.* 21, 27. As early as 1782 Archdeacon Paley had pointed to "the competition of opposite analogies" as one cause of the uncertainty of justice. *Moral and Political Philosophy,* bk. vi, chap. viii (quoted by A. L. Goodhart in work cited in n. 40, *supra*).

Two evidently opposed maxims are *"sic utere tuo ut alienum non laedas"* and *"qui jure suo utitur neminem laedit"* (D. 50, 17, 151, and 155, § 1). See Broom's *Legal Maxims* (8th Am. ed.), 366* and 379*. For the comparable situation in Continental law, see K. G. Wurzel, "Methods of Juridical Thinking," *Science of Legal Methods* (Boston, 1917), pp. 300–328.

52. *Am. Charters,* etc. (Thorpe, ed.), VII, 3816–3817.

53. Carl Schmitt, *Die Diktatur von den Anfängen des modernen Souveränitäts-gedanken,* etc. (Munich and Leipzig, 1928), contains a reminder to this effect. "Energy in the executive is a leading character in the definition of good government. . . . Every man the least conversant in Roman story, knows how often that republic was obliged to take refuge in the absolute power of a single man, under the formidable title of Dictator. . . ." Hamilton in *Federalist 70* (Lodge ed., p. 436).

Notes 219

54. (Second) *Treatise on Civil Government* (Morley, ed.), chap. xii.

55. *Ibid.*, chap. xiv.

56. Farrand (ed.), *Records,* I, 65; see also *ibid.,* pp. 68 and 85, and II, 29.

57. Hamilton and the younger Pinckney were also of this group, as was Madison to a less extent.

58. Their views can be readily traced through the index to Farrand's *Records.*

59. Farrand, *op. cit.,* II, 52–54 (July, 19).

60. *Ibid.,* III, 419–420.

61. *Ibid.,* II, 171, 185, 398.

62. 1 *Annals of Cong.* 480–481.

63. *Messages and Papers,* III, 79–80.

64. Bruce Wyman, *Administrative Law* (St. Paul, 1903), p. 233.

65. 12 Pet. 524 at 610 (1838).

66. 272 U.S. at 135.

67. Mr. Humphrey's death makes it uncertain whether the action he had started in the Court of Claims will be continued. Myer's action was prosecuted through its final stages by his widow.

68. 1 Cr. at 165–166.

69. The material part of the discussion is given in my *President's Control of Foreign Relations* (Princeton, 1917), pp. 7–28.

70. "Of these [the three branches] the legislative . . is by far the most important." President Monroe, "Views of the President, etc.," *Messages and Papers,* II, 150. "The legislative is the only creative element in our government, and precedes the other departments, inasmuch as they only act upon that which the legislative power has brought into existence." Argument of counsel in 17 How. 284 at 296. See also citation in n. 65, *supra,* and 3 How. at 245.

71. 1 *Opins. A.G.* 631; 2 *ibid.* 525.

72. F. W. Maitland, *The Constitutional History of England* (Cambridge, 1908), p. 299.

73. *Messages and Papers,* VI, 23, 30–31.

74. J. G. Randall, *Constitutional Problems under Lincoln* (New York, 1926), pp. 378, 514.

75. 2 Bl. 635 (1863).

76. 4 Wall. 2 (1866).

77. *Ibid.* at 81.

78. 12 Wall. 457 (1871).

79. Sidney George Fisher, in his learned and penetrating volume *The Trial of the Constitution* (Philadelphia, 1862), attributed to the national government as a whole all necessary powers for its own preservation. "What a government can do, and ought to do, is the law of that government," *ibid.*, p. 95. He also claimed for the President corresponding powers when Congress was not in session, subject to later disallowance by Congress on the principle that "the Executive is subordinate to the Legislature," *ibid.*, p. 216. See generally *ibid.*, chaps. i and iii. They are of great interest today.

80. In addition to the Legal Tender cases, cited n. 78 *supra*, see *Am. Ins. Co.* v. *Canter*, 1 Pet. 511 (1828); *United States* v. *Kagama*. 118 U.S. 375 (1886); *United States* v. *Arjona*, 120 U.S. 479 (1887); *Jones* v. *U.S.*, 137 U.S. 202 (1890); *Ekiu* v. *U.S.*, 142 U.S. 651 (1892); *Fong Yue Ting* v. *U.S.*, 149 U.S. 698 (1893).

81. *Missouri* v. *Holland*, 252 U.S. 416 at 433. In his sagacious work *Constitutional Power and World Affairs* (New York, 1919), written before he ascended the Bench, Justice Sutherland argues that the national government has complete power in the field of foreign affairs. Referring to the Tenth Amendment, he says: "In thus parcelling out the totality of political power, it must be assumed that the intention was to vest in one government or the other [i.e., in the national government or the states], every power the exercise of which would contribute to the usefulness of government as an agency to promote the public good, and to withhold only such as, for sound reasons of public policy, ought not to be vested in any government. . . . The state governments . . . are confined in their operations to their own boundaries, and from the nature and structure of our governmental system, as well as by the prohibitions of the Constitution, they can exercise no power externally. It follows, then, that the reservation to the respective states can have no reference to any power externally, but refers to internal power exclusively, and that every power over external affairs, not vested in the general government, is held in reserve by the people, and therefore, incapable of practical exercise." The comment I wish to make is that, inasmuch as "the state governments *are* confined in their operations to their own boundaries," they are just as incompetent to exercise *internal* powers of

government which require to be exercised on a national scale as they are to exercise powers in the field of foreign relations; and that Justice Sutherland's argument is, therefore, equally valid to prove that the national government should be credited with all the powers of *internal* government that could be beneficially exercised on a national scale. This, in fact, was precisely the argument used by James Wilson in 1782 in support of the right of the Congress of the Confederation to charter the Bank of North America. Reciting the second of the Articles of Confederation, "each state retains its sovereignty . . . and every power . . . which is not, by the Confederation expressly delegated to the United States in Congress assembled," Wilson answered: "But, we presume, it will not be contended, that any or each of the states, could exercise any power or act of sovereignty extending over all the other states, or any of them." The Articles of Confederation, therefore, he proceeded, did not apply to the case: "For many purposes, the United States are to be considered as one undivided, independent nation, and as possessed of all the rights, and powers, and properties, by the law of nations incident to such." *The Works of James Wilson* (Andrews, ed. Chicago, 1896), I, 556–558. That the reservation in the Ninth and Tenth amendments, to "the people" of certain rights and powers make them exercisable by the national government in case of grave necessity, has been argued. See the opinion of Judge Campbell in *Van Husen* v. *Kanouse,* 13 Mich. 313 (1864); also an article by Judge Wm. H. Black, of New York State Supreme Court, 1st District, in *Christian Science Monitor,* May 19, 1934, p. 14.

82. February term of 1790; 2 Dall. 399–400.

83. See 3 Wheat. 172 (1818); 5 Pet. 115 (1831); 10 Pet. 343 (1836); 15 Pet. 290 (1841); 104 U.S. 444 (1881); 125 U.S. 273 (1888).

84. 5 Pet. at 122.

85. 6 *Opins. A.G.* 466. See also *ibid.* at 28 and 220.

86. *In re Neagle,* 135 U.S. 1.

87. *Ibid.* at 64 and 69.

88. 158 U.S. 564.

89. *Ibid.* at 586.

90. *Our Chief Magistrate and His Powers* (Columbia Univ., 1916), p. 97.

91. *An Autobiography* (New York, 1913), pp. 388–389.

92. *Op. cit.,* pp. 138–140. Mr. Taft quotes A. P. Upshur, a

member of Tyler's Cabinet, as saying, in the course of a criticism of Story's *Commentaries:* "We have heard it gravely asserted in Congress that whatever power is neither legislative nor judiciary, is of course executive, and, as such, belongs to the President under the Constitution." Another statement of the residual power theory which attracted much attention at the time was that of Senator Works of California in the Senate, January 5, 1917; see *Cong. Record* of that date.

93. For the sources of the above quoted passages see Frankfurter and Davison, *Cases and Other Materials on Administrative Law* (Chicago, 1932), pp. 459–464, reproducing the opening section of the excellent article by Patrick Duff and H. E. Whiteside, *"Delegata Potestas non Potest Delegari:* A maxim of American Constitutional Law," 14 *Corn. L.Q.* 168 ff. (1929).

94. *Op. cit.,* chap. xi (Morley, ed., p. 266).

95. See chap. ii, p. 68, *supra.*

96. 38 Minn. 281 at 301 (1888); quoted with approval by C.J. Taft in *J. W. Hampton, Jr. and Co.* v. *U.S.,* 276 U.S. 394 at 408 (1928). "If Congress were required to fix every [railroad] rate, it would be impossible to exercise the right at all." *Ibid.,* 407. In other words, the release of legislative power from the maxim has meant the practical strengthening of such power, not its weakening. "It is proved by a half century of experience that the tariff can not be reviewed by Congress more than once in seven or eight years. It is only a destruction of the principle of the flexible tariff to provide that the Commission's recommendations should be made to Congress for action instead of the Executive." President Hoover, 71 *Cong. Rec.* 4080 (September 30, 1929), quoted in Frankfurter and Davison, *op. cit.* in n. 93, *supra,* at p. 489.

97. 192 U.S. 470 (1904).

98. *Ibid.* at 496. See also *United States* v. *Grimaud,* 220 U.S. 506 (1911). The President can also obtain power simply by exercising it with the silent acquiescence of Congress through a course of years. See *United States* v. *Midwest Oil Co.,* 236 U.S. 459 (1915).

99. 242 U.S. 311 (1917).

100. *Ibid.* at 326.

101. See John Dickinson, *op. cit.,* n. 12, *supra,* chap. xi.

102. Carl McFarland, *Judicial Control of the Federal Trade Commission and the Interstate Commerce Commission, 1920–1930.* (Harvard Univ., 1933), chap. v. The question arises

whether Congress could effectively forbid the Federal courts
to entertain suits for injunction against national administrative
officers. It is established doctrine, and has been from the beginning of the government, that, in the words of Justice
Sutherland, "every other court [except the Supreme Court]
created by the general government derives its jurisdiction
wholly from the authority of Congress." *Kline* v. *Burke Construction Co.*, 260 U.S. 226 at 234 (1922). To the same effect is
Turner v. *B'k. of N.A.*, 4 Dall. 8, 10 (1799). Meantime, Justice
Story had contributed the beginnings of another theory, in the
contention that there are cases which Congress cannot constitutionally withhold from Federal jurisdiction, among them being suits against officers charged with exceeding their authority. 3 How. 236 at 252–260 (1845). Also the argument is
offered that when a "case"—in the sense of litigation—is submitted at all to a Federal court, it is submitted without restriction to a tribunal which, by the terms of the Constitution
is a court of law and equity, and hence is vested in the latter
capacity with the full powers of the English Court of Chan-
cery. The recent decision in *Crowell* v. *Benson,* 285 U.S. 22
(1932), seems to show that the Court today accepts this line of
reasoning as having considerable validity for cases involving
constitutional rights. The whole subject is competently treated
in an unpublished thesis by Dr. Robert J. Harris, Princeton
Univ. Ph.D., 1934. The thesis is on file in the University Library.

103. The collapse of 1929 and succeeding depression evoked
not a few programs pivoting upon the idea of a Presidential
dictatorship—a phenomenon which has pretty generally ceased
since Mr. Roosevelt came into office. An illustration—a rather
extreme one, to be sure—is furnished by the article of Mr.
Ralph Adams Cram reprinted in the Boston *Globe* of July 16,
1932, from *The Commonweal.* The title of the article is "A
Motion to Suspend the Constitution" and this title is well lived
up to. The essence of the proposal is that the President should
get rid of Congress and proceed to rule with a "council of
state," which should take such measures as appeared to them
necessary "to save the Republic from catastrophe and restore
a measure of order and confidence." Appropriations would be
thus reduced, the income tax lowered, the Eighteenth Amendment repealed, and so on—anything that Mr. Cram wished at
the time to see done. Then an election would be called, and if

it went against the President he would voluntarily surrender himself to the courts and "accept without complaint such disposition of himself as might be determined upon."

Interesting, too, in this general connection is the following extract from the Summary of the Report of the President's Committee on Recent Social Trends: "The power to act within the three-fold separation of governmental authorities likewise shows the emergence of centralized power, and the forecast indicates still further development toward the central focus of authority." "The executive has gained in prestige and power in the national and State governments, and in some cities where the power of the mayor has been expanded. . . . The familiarity of the public with the 'strong man' with large authority in business and social relations has also helped in this movement. The almost omnipotent legislative authority set up at the outset of our national development has steadily lost to the courts on the one side and the executive on the other; and this process has gone on more rapidly than ever during recent years. . . . Yet the maxim, 'It is the function of many to deliberate and of one to act,' contains the essence of much past experience and wisdom of government, under a variety of different systems, and it seems probable that representative bodies will occupy places of power and distinction in the organization of society, under any development of executive power or administrative authority." *New York Times,* January 2, 1933.

The question of the future of the Presidency may also be considered in the light of the contemporary breakdown of Parliamentarism in Europe. "L'Exécutif irresponsable, l'exécutif personnel, c'est la dictature. L'Exécutif fort, l'Exécutif creatur, l'Exécutif puissant, c'est la nécessité technique de la démocratie": "La primauté politique de l'Exécutif," by Professor B. Mirkine-Guetzevitch, in *Revue Internationale de la Théorie du Droit,* V, 1–14, at p. 14. And see further Professor Herbert Kraus, *The Crisis of German Democracy* (Princeton, 1932), chap. ix. Oswald Spengler, in *The Hour of Decision* (New York, 1934), argues that democracy is bound presently to give way to dictatorship everywhere; but this conclusion is tied up with the idea that the Marxian doctrine of "class struggle" is everywhere held by the laboring class, which is certainly not the case in this country.

CHAPTER IV

1. *Messages and Papers of the Presidents,* VIII, 557. Many years earlier, in his Message of September 4, 1837, to a special session of Congress, President Van Buren had written: "Those who look to the action of this government for specific aid to the citizen to relieve embarrassments arising from losses by revulsions in commerce and credit lose sight of the ends for which it was created. . . . It is not its legitimate object to make men rich or to repair by direct grants of money or by legislation in favor of particular pursuits losses not incurred in the public service." *Ibid.,* III, 344–345.

2. The following pages are in the main taken from my article on "The Spending Power of Congress," 36 *Harv. L.R.* 548–582 (March, 1923), with the consent of the editors of that publication. For other details and a somewhat different emphasis, see Charles Warren's interesting little volume, *Congress as Santa Claus* (Charlottesville, 1932).

3. See Story, *Comms.,* §§ 907, 908, and references; Farrand, *Records,* III, 379; J. Q. Adams, *Memoirs,* VI, 121–127; *Writings of James Madison* (Hunt, ed.), IX, 411–424 (Letter of November 27, 1830 to Speaker Stevenson).

4. Story, *op. cit.,* § 908 and references.

5. J. Q. Adams, *loc cit.;* Madison, *loc. cit.,* 413 n.

6. 272 U.S. at 118 and 128.

7. *The General Welfare Clause* (set, stereotyped, printed and copyrighted by the author, Washington, D.C., 1926, 388 pp.). A revised edition has recently appeared which I have not seen. It appears that a certain M. L. Hulbert wrote a pamphlet urging this same view of the "general welfare" clause and sent a copy of it to Madison, in 1830. See Madison's letter to Hulbert, *op. cit.,* IX, 370–375. See also *Cong. Record* for May 9, 1933, pp. 3142–3153.

8. For a further expression of the Madisonian doctrine, see *Messages and Papers,* I, 584–585; and *Writings* (Hunt, ed.), VI, 356–357. "The general welfare that is to be provided for is the general welfare of the government in all those matters of which it has special cognizance and in respect of which its efficiency concerns the whole country." G. T. Curtis, *History of the Constitution* (New York, 1897), II, 592. The argument is here advanced that the term "United States" in the Constitu-

tion means the United States *government,* which seems to over-
look the opening words of the document!

9. *Op. cit.* § 924.

10. Letters cited in nn. 3 and 7, *supra.*

11. *Works* (Lodge, ed.), IV, 70 ff.

12. *Ibid.,* p. 151.

13. Benton's *Abridg.,* I, 350 ff.

14. *Messages and Papers,* I, 201–202.

15. *Writings,* VI, 355–356.

16. *American State Papers* (Miscel.) II, 443. For the Supreme Court's rejection of the doctrine of state consent following the Civil War, see *Kohl* v. *U.S.,* 91 U.S. 367 (1875).

17. The early history of internal improvements is sufficiently
sketched in Monroe's "Views of the President, etc." of May 4,
1822, *Messages and Papers,* II, 169–171.

18. Benton, *Abridg.,* V, 706–707.

19. See n. 8, *supra.* Although the House failed to override the
veto, the vote in favor of doing so was sixty yeas to fifty-six
nays, while among the "yeas" were Webster, Clay, and Calhoun.

20. *Messages and Papers,* II, 18.

21. *Am. St. Papers* (Miscel.) II, 443 ff.; *Annals of Congress,*
XXXI, 451 ff. (15th Cong., 1st sess.).

22. *Messages and Papers,* II, 144–183.

23. *Ibid.,* pp. 157–173, *passim.*

24. *Ibid.,* pp. 294–299.

25. *Ibid.,* pp. 299–317. The passages quoted are from pp. 311–
317.

26. *Ibid.,* pp. 483–493. For other vetoes see pp. 493, 508, 638.

27. *Ibid.,* III, 120–121.

28. *Ibid.,* p. 122.

29. *Ibid.,* IV, 330, 460 ff., 616–617; V, 20, 90, 218 ff., 259 ff.
Buchanan recurred to Madison's and Polk's views. *Ibid.,* pp.
601 ff. Later vetoes of rivers and harbors bills have not raised
the general constitutional question, but have invoked the distinction between national and local improvements. *Ibid.,* VII,
382; VIII, 120; IX, 677.

30. *Ibid.,* V, 220, 457, 526, 570, 650. Taylor and Fillmore had
recommended the enterprise earlier, but with little reference to
the constitutional question. *Ibid.,* pp. 20 and 86. In sustaining, in
1888, the constitutionality of the acts of 1862 and 1864, charter-
ing the Union Pacific and Central Pacific lines, the Court in-

voked not only the war power but the commerce and postal powers as well. 127 U.S. 1.

31. W. L. Wanlass, *United States Department of Agriculture* (Johns Hopkins Univ., 1920), *passim.* The department was originally headed by a Commissioner. In 1889 it became an Executive Department, whose head, a Secretary, was admitted to the Cabinet.

32. *Messages and Papers,* V, 543.

33. *Ibid.,* pp. 547–549.

34. 12 *Stat. at L.* 503, c. 130.

35. *Messages and Papers,* VII, 152, 203, 606, 626; VIII, 58.

36. 26 *Stat. at L.* 417.

37. *Messages and Papers,* VIII, 143, 184, 253.

38. D. R. Dewey, *National Problems* ("The American Nation; a History," Vol. XXIV), pp. 89–90.

39. 31 *Stat. at L.* 179, c. 479.

40. 34 *Stat. at L.* 1281, c. 2907.

41. 38 *Stat. at L.* 372, c. 79.

42. 39 *Stat. at L.* 929, c. 114.

43. 41 *Stat. at L.* 715, c. 219. See also the Act of March 3, 1879, c. 186, 26 *Stat. at L.* 468; and the Act of June 25, 1906, .c. 3536, 34 *Stat. at L.* 460. The former appropriated $250,000 "out of money in the United States Treasury not otherwise appropriated," as a perpetual fund for the purpose of aiding the education of the blind, through the American Printing House for the Blind, located at Louisville, Kentucky. The latter commuted the income from this fund with an annual appropriation of $10,000. Note, too, the Act of July 1, 1898, c. 546, 30 *Stat. at L.* 624, for an appropriation to Howard University, with conditions attached.

44. 44 *Stat. at L.,* c. 135, p. 224.

45. On the general subject of "federal grants in aid," see Austin F. MacDonald, *Federal Subsidies* (New York, 1928); and Paul V. Betters, "Federal Services to Municipal Governments," *Public Administration Service,* Report No. 24.

46. Cited n. 30, *supra;* see also *Luxton* v. *No. R. Bridge Co.,* 153 U.S. 525 (1894).

47. 160 U.S. 668 (1896).

48. *Smith* v. *Kansas City Title and Trust Co.,* 255 U.S. 180. The case was twice argued, and finally decided by a divided Court.

49. A minor feature of Mr. Hughes's brief invites a word of

comment. At one point he cites the "disposing" clause of Art. IV, § 3, p. 2 ("The Congress shall have power to dispose of . . . property belonging to the United States"), and appears to argue that even if the "taxing" clauses do not give Congress power to appropriate money for "the general welfare," this clause does. The argument is superfluous. The power to tax infers necessarily the power and *duty* of the taxing body to devote the resulting funds to the general welfare. Without this purpose in view there is no taxing power.

50. *Massachusetts* v. *Mellon* and *Frothingham* v. *Mellon*, 262 U.S. 447.

51. See the elaborate briefs in the *Report*.

52. 262 U.S. at 485–486. Cf., however, *Missouri* v. *Holland*, 252 U.S. 416.

53. 262 U.S. at 487–488. The opinion continues: "If one taxpayer may champion and litigate such a cause, then every other taxpayer may do the same . . . in respect of every . . . appropriation act and statute whose administration requires the outlay of money, and whose validity may be challenged. The bare suggestion . . . goes far to sustain the conclusion which we have reached, that a suit of this character cannot be maintained. It is of much significance that no precedent sustaining the right to maintain suits like this has been called to our attention, although, since the formation of the government . . . a large number of statutes appropriating or involving the expenditure of moneys for nonfederal purposes have been enacted and carried into effect."

54. *Van Brocklin* v. *Tenn.*, 117 U.S. 151 (1885).

55. *Camfield* v. *U.S.*, 167 U.S. 518 (1897).

56. Cited n. 47, *supra*.

57. For a spirited and informed defense of various national services against much biased criticism, see Dr. T. Swann Harding's TNT, *Those National Tax-eaters* (New York, 1934), *passim*.

RÉSUMÉ

1. Charles Evans Hughes, *Addresses* (New York, 1908), p. 139.

2. *Reflections on the Revolution in France, etc.* (Everyman's Lib., 1929), pp. 19–20.

3. *Culture and Anarchy* (New York, 1912), pp. 70–71. Ba-

con's words also are pertinent: "He that will not apply new remedies must expect new evils, for time is the greatest innovator. . . . A froward retention of custom is as turbulent a thing as an innovation." *Essays,* "Innovations." One does not have to have a vision of Utopia to be able to perceive the necessity, under modern conditions, for constantly reshaping our institutions.

4. 110 U.S. at 530–531.
5. 288 U.S. at 360.

INDEX

(This index is incomplete for the cases mentioned in the Notes.)

Date Due